# GIFTS ANL ~~CALLING~~

## TARGETING YOUR PASSION

General Editor
LYMAN COLEMAN

Managing Editor
DENISE BELTZNER

Assistant Editors
DOUGLAS LABUDDE
KEITH MADSEN

Cover Art
CHRISTOPHER WERNER

Cover Design
ERICA TIEPEL

Layout Production
FRONTLINE GROUP

*Reference Notes* by Richard Peace, ©1984, 1985, 1986, Serendipity House.

## Seven Keys to a Highly Energized Life

| Session | Track One | Track Two |
|---|---|---|
| 1 ORIENTATION | Called by God: Mt. 4:18–22; 9:9 | |
| 2 HEARING GOD'S CALL | Called in a New Direction: Ac. 16:6–10 | Called to a New Life: 1 Cor. 1:26–31 |
| 3 FINDING YOUR GIFT | A Division of Duties: Ac. 6:1–7 | A Variety of Gifts: 1 Cor. 12:7–27 |
| 4 TAKING THE RISK | The Risk of Investment: Mt. 25:14–30 | No More Timidity: 2 Tim. 1:3–14 |
| 5 THE ROLE OF MONEY | True Treasure: Mt. 6:19–24 | A Root of Evil: 1 Tim. 6:3–10 |
| 6 OUR ATTITUDE TOWARD WORK | Stewards in Our Work: Mt. 21:33–41 | Submission to Our Task: 1 Pet. 2:13–21 |
| 7 THE SERVANT MIND | An Example of Servanthood: Jn. 13:2–17 | Taking On Servanthood: Php. 2:3–11 |

Serendipity / Box 1012 / Littleton, CO 80160    (800)525-9563

FOUR THINGS YOU NEED TO KNOW ABOUT

# Beginning a Small Group

**1. PURPOSE:** This course is designed for 101 groups to continue. The goal is to get better acquainted and become a support group. We call this the "formation period" of a group or 201. Using the analogy of a baseball diamond, the goal is home plate or "bonding." To get to home plate, the group needs to go around

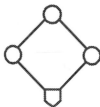 three bases: FIRST BASE: History Giving—telling your "story" to one another—your childhood, your journey, your hopes and dreams. SECOND BASE: Affirmation—responding to each other's story with appreciation. THIRD BASE: Need Sharing—going deeper in your story—your present struggles, roadblocks, anxieties, and where you need help from God and the group.

**2. AGENDA:** There are three parts to every group meeting:

| GATHERING / 10 min. | BIBLE STUDY / 30 min. | CARING / 20 min. |
|---|---|---|
| Purpose: To break the ice and become better acquainted | Purpose: To share your spiritual journey | Purpose: To share prayer requests and pray |

**3. FEARLESS FOURSOME:** If you have more than 7 in your group at any time, call the option play when the time comes for Bible study, and subdivide into groups of 4 for greater participation. (In 4's, everyone will share and you can finish the Bible study in 30 minutes.) Then regather the group for the Caring Time.

| GATHERING | BIBLE STUDY | CARING |
|---|---|---|
| All Together | Groups of 4 | Back Together |

**4. EMPTY CHAIR:** Pull up an empty chair during the **Caring Time** at the close and ask God to fill this chair each week. Remember, by breaking into groups of four for the Bible study time, you can grow numerically without feeling "too big" as a group.

The Group Leader needs an Apprentice in training at all times so that the Apprentice can start a new "cell" when the group size is twelve or more.

# INSTRUCTIONS FOR GROUP LEADER

**PURPOSE:** **What is this course all about?** Within a supportive group relationship, to discover our calling and how we can best use our talents in fulfilling our calling.

**SEEKERS/ STRUGGLERS:** **Who is this course designed for?** Two kinds of people: (a) Seekers who do not know where they are with God but are open to finding out, and (b) Strugglers who are committed to Jesus Christ, but want to grow in their faith.

**NEW PEOPLE:** **Does this mean I can invite my non-church friends?** Absolutely. In fact, this would be a good place for people on their way back to God to start.

**STUDY:** **What are we going to study?** The focus of this course is to help us search together for our calling, and how we can use the gifts the Spirit has given us in that calling (see title page). The rest of the agenda is outlined on page 2.

**FIRST SESSION:** **What do we do at the meetings?** In the first session, you get acquainted and decide on the Ground Rules for your group. In sessions two through seven, you have the option of two Tracks for Bible study.

**TWO TRACKS:** **What are the two tracks?** TRACK ONE—This study is best for newly-formed groups or groups that are unfamiliar with small group Bible study. This option primarily contains multiple-choice questions, with no "right or wrong" answers.

TRACK TWO—This study is best for groups who have had previous small group Bible studies and want to dig deeper into the Scriptures. The questions are deeper—and the Scripture is a teaching passage.

**CHOOSING A TRACK:** **Which track of Bible study do you recommend?** The TRACK ONE study is best for newly-formed groups, groups that are unfamiliar with small group Bible study, or groups that are only meeting for an hour. The TRACK TWO study is best for deeper Bible study groups, or groups which meet for more than an hour.

**CHOOSING BOTH TRACKS:** **Can we choose both tracks?** If your group meets for 90 to 120 minutes, you can choose to do both studies at the same time. Or you can spend two weeks on a unit—TRACK ONE the first week and TRACK TWO the next. Or you can do one of the tracks in the meeting and the other track for homework.

**SMALL GROUP:** **What is different about this course?** It is written for a small group to do together.

**GROUP BUILDING:** **What is the purpose behind your approach to Bible study?** To give everyone a chance to share their own "spiritual story," and to bond as a group. This is often referred to as "koinonia."

**KOINONIA:** **What is koinonia and why is it a part of these studies?** Koinonia means "fellowship." It is an important part of these sessions, because as a group gets to know one another, they are more willing to share their needs and care for one another.

**BIBLE KNOWLEDGE:** **What if I don't know much about the Bible?** No problem. Track One is based on a Bible story that stands on its own—to discuss as though you were hearing it for the first time. Plus there are a few Reference Notes to point out important details. Track Two comes with Comments and complete Reference Notes—to keep you up to speed.

**COMMENTS & REFERENCE NOTES:** **What is the purpose of the Comments and Reference Notes in the studies?** To help you understand the context of the Bible passage and any difficult words that need to be defined.

**LEADERSHIP:** **Who leads the meetings?** Ideally, there should be three people: (a) trained leader, (b) apprentice or co-leader, and (c) host. Having an apprentice-in-training in the group, you have a built-in system for multiplying the group if it gets too large. In fact, this is one of the goals of the group—to give "birth" to a new group in time.

**RULES:** **What are the ground rules for the group?**

**Priority:** While you are in the course, you give the group meetings priority.

**Participation:** Everyone participates and no one dominates.

**Respect:** Everyone is given the right to their own opinion, and "dumb questions" are encouraged and respected.

**Confidentiality:** Anything that is said in the meeting is never repeated outside the meeting.

**Empty Chair:** The group stays open to new people at every meeting as long as they understand the ground rules.

**Support:** Permission is given to call upon each other in time of need at any time.

**Continuing:** What happens to the group after finishing this course? The group is free to disband or continue to another course. (See page 62 for making a Covenant and continuing together as a group.)

## SESSION 1

# Orientation

**PURPOSE:** To get acquainted, to share your expectations, and to decide on the ground rules for your group.

**AGENDA:** ⟳ Gathering ⌒ Bible Study ♡ Caring Time

## GATHERING / 10 Minutes / All Together

*Leader: The purpose of the Gathering time is to break the ice. Read the instructions for Step One and go first. Then read the Introduction (Step Two) and the instructions for the Bible study. If you are not familiar with the Scripture, read the Reference Notes at the close of the session.*

**OPEN**

**Step One: THE OLD NEIGHBORHOOD.** During this course of study, our efforts at *becoming* a sharing community will be rooted in our histories of *being* part of a community. Let's begin by looking at your "old neighborhood." If you moved a lot, talk about the neighborhood where you spent the most time, or the one which was your favorite. Share your name, the name of the town where you were raised, and your responses to the following:

1. Was your "old neighborhood" more like:
   - ❑ *Sesame Street*—urban and multicultural
   - ❑ Bill Cosby's neighborhood—distinctively ethnic
   - ❑ *Leave it to Beaver*—suburban housing with a common cultural background
   - ❑ *The Waltons*—rural and spread out, but close-knit

2. Share your responses to as many of the following as you have time for:
   - ❑ where did the kids gather in your neighborhood?
   - ❑ what were your favorite activities to do together?
   - ❑ where were the special places—the best climbing trees, the best swimming holes? the places you could go to hide from adults? the homes which gave the best Halloween treats?
   - ❑ where were the "danger spots"—the yards with mean dogs, the "Oscar the Grouches" who didn't like kids, the "haunted" houses?
   - ❑ who were the kids who really stood out from the rest of the crowd—the "Weird Harolds" and "Eddie Haskells"?

**Step Two: WELCOME.** Welcome to a group where together we will seek community while we explore the topic of our "gifts and calling." We won't be the "old neighborhood," but rather new neighbors who celebrate an old value of caring for each other.

Our gifts and calling are central elements of our uniqueness as people. Our gifts are the specific, Spirit-given abilities which enable us to contribute to the wider good of the community and world. Our calling is the task or area of service where God directs us to use those gifts. Our calling is sometimes called our "vocation." At times, that word is too closely identified with a paid job. Our calling may or may not be the same thing as our paid job. Sometimes a calling is something we need to do as a volunteer.

*"Vocation is the response a person makes with his or her total self to the address of God and to the calling of partnership."*
*—James Fowler*

It can be difficult for many of us to determine our calling. How do we know what God is calling us to do? Some people have a strong sense of this in high school; others do not discover it until well into adulthood. Former tennis great Arthur Ashe (who died in 1993 from AIDS) was looking for his vocation *after* his tennis career was over, and even after he contracted AIDS (from a blood transfusion). He wrote in his book *Days of Grace*: "If God hadn't put me on this earth mainly to stroke tennis balls, he certainly hadn't put me here to be greedy. I wanted to make a difference, however small, in the world, and I wanted to do so in a useful and honorable way."

According to a survey done by James Patterson and Peter Kim for their book *The Day America Told the Truth*, many people do not see their present work as a true vocation. Consider these statistics from that survey:

- Only 1 in 4 people work to achieve their potential rather than to merely keep the wolf from the door
- Only 1 in 4 people give work their best effort
- Only 1 in 10 say they are satisfied with their jobs
- Almost half of American workers admit to chronic malingering (calling in sick when they are not sick, and doing it regularly)

The central focus of this course is to help us search together for our calling, and how we can use the gifts the Spirit has given us in that calling.

Every session has three parts: (1) **Gathering**—to break the ice and introduce the topic, (2) **Bible study**—to share your own study through a passage of Scripture, and (3) **Caring**—to decide what action you need to take in this area of your life and to support one another in this action.

In this course, we want to learn about the Bible, but we want to do so in a way that sheds light on who we are. The focus, then, will be on telling your story and using the passage as a springboard.

# BIBLE STUDY / 30 Minutes / Groups of 4

*Leader: If you have more than 7 in this session, we recommend groups of four—4 to sit around the dining table, 4 around the kitchen table, and 4 around a folding table. Ask one person in each foursome to be the Convener and complete the Bible study in the time allowed. Then regather for the Caring Time, allowing 20 minutes.*

**STUDY**

In each foursome, ask someone to be the Convener. These verses are from the beginning of Jesus' ministry, and they focus on the calling of his closest supporters in ministry. Read Matthew 4:18–22 and 9:9. Go around on the first question. Then go around with the next question, and work your way through the questionnaire. After 30 minutes, the Leader will call time and ask you to regather for the Caring Time. If you have any questions about difficult words or phrases, consult the Reference Notes on page 11.

> **¹⁸ As Jesus was walking beside the Sea of Galilee, he saw two brothers, Simon called Peter and his brother Andrew. They were casting a net into the lake, for they were fishermen. ¹⁹ "Come, follow me," Jesus said, "and I will make you fishers of men." ²⁰ At once they left their nets and followed him.**
>
> **²¹ Going on from there, he saw two other brothers, James son of Zebedee and his brother John. They were in a boat with their father Zebedee, preparing their nets. Jesus called them, ²² and immediately they left the boat and their father and followed him.**
>
> **⁹ As Jesus went on from there, he saw a man named Matthew sitting at the tax collector's booth. "Follow me," he told him, and Matthew got up and followed him.**
>
> *Matthew 4:18–22; 9:9, NIV*

1. What is your first reaction to Jesus' style of calling these disciples?
   - ❏ it seems pretty random and slipshod
   - ❏ it seems arrogant to ask total strangers to follow you
   - ❏ it seems he knew exactly what he was doing and why he was doing it
   - ❏ Jesus knew whoever he asked would respond

*"It never cost disciple anything to follow Jesus: to talk about cost when you are in love with someone is an insult."
—Oswald Chambers*

2. Why do you think Jesus chose these particular people?
   - ❏ these were random choices
   - ❏ he chose a representative sample—like a Gallup poll
   - ❏ he knew them better than they knew themselves and chose them based on that knowledge
   - ❏ he saw how hard they were working
   - ❏ having met them before, he knew there was good "chemistry" between them
   - ❏ he had supernatural insight into their potential

3. Why did the disciples respond so quickly to Jesus' call?
   - ❒ they were bored with what they were doing
   - ❒ they really had no choice
   - ❒ they had already "applied for the job" and Jesus was announcing the "hiring list"
   - ❒ they recognized Jesus' authority and trustworthiness
   - ❒ they were curious
   - ❒ they were immediately drawn by Jesus' personality
   - ❒ they heard the truth from Jesus and recognized it
   - ❒ other: _____

4. When was the first time you remember feeling God's call on your life?
   - ❒ when I was a child
   - ❒ when I was in trouble
   - ❒ when I was away on retreat
   - ❒ when I was all alone
   - ❒ when I faced death
   - ❒ all my life
   - ❒ just recently
   - ❒ never

5. Imagine that you are embarking on a multi-year project to change people's attitudes and make a difference in the world. What qualities would you look for in the persons you choose to work with you? (Pick the top three.)
   - ❒ a strong work ethic
   - ❒ a good sense of humor
   - ❒ creativity
   - ❒ an even temper
   - ❒ loyalty
   - ❒ dedication to the cause
   - ❒ intelligence
   - ❒ a love for people
   - ❒ the ability to follow
   - ❒ the ability to lead
   - ❒ honesty
   - ❒ they would have to like me
   - ❒ patience
   - ❒ charisma

6. If you asked Jesus to consider you for such a team of disciples, which three strengths would you list first on your résumé? (Choose from the list above, or add your own.)

7. When you were in the seventh grade, what was your vision of what you wanted to be when you grew up? If that vision changed, what changed it?

8. If Jesus came to your place of work tomorrow and said, "follow me" (like he did with these first disciples), what would your response be?
   - ❒ I think you're talking to the wrong person
   - ❒ can you wait until I'm on break?
   - ❒ I can't afford a job change right now
   - ❒ I thought I was following you already
   - ❒ sure—but can't I stay here and do it?
   - ❒ tell me what you want, and I'll do it
   - ❒ other: _____

9. When it comes to Jesus' invitation to "come and follow," are you:
   ❏ still checking out Jesus on the basis of someone else's recommendation?
   ❏ going after him to get to know him yourself?
   ❏ eager to invite others to join you in your journey with Jesus?
   ❏ skeptical that there really is anything to this business?
   ❏ overwhelmed with the insight Jesus has of you?
   ❏ other: _____

10. Which of the following best describes your present attitude toward what you are doing in life?
    ❏ I'm working to live
    ❏ I'm living to work
    ❏ my true vocation is not in the area of my paid work
    ❏ I'm searching for a true vocation—something that's more than a paycheck
    ❏ God could use me in a meaningful way in the work I'm doing now—if I let him
    ❏ God has called me to my present job, and I get satisfaction from that
    ❏ I just need a job—any job

11. In order to better understand and carry out your calling, what do you most need from these sessions together?
    ❏ someone to search with me
    ❏ someone to bounce around crazy ideas with
    ❏ someone to help me understand God's direction
    ❏ someone to help me see my strengths more clearly
    ❏ a vision from God
    ❏ other: _____

12. How would you characterize your follow-through on your call to be a disciple?
    ❏ Jesus is my Lord, and I follow him daily
    ❏ Jesus is a great rabbi (teacher): I listen, but follow when I like
    ❏ Jesus is my Savior, but we don't have a close relationship
    ❏ Jesus is the Son of God, but not too involved in my daily life
    ❏ Jesus is my Messiah, and I'm here to find out what that means
    ❏ other: _____

# CARING TIME / 20 Minutes / All Together

*Leader: In this first session, take some time to discuss your Expectations and to decide on the Ground Rules for your group. Then spend the remaining time in caring support for each other through Sharing and Prayer.*

1. What motivated you to come to this group?
   ❏ curiosity
   ❏ a friend asked me
   ❏ I had nothing better to do
   ❏ a nagging suspicion that I better get my life together

**EXPECTATIONS**

2. As you begin this group, what are some goals or expectations you have for this course? Choose two or three of the following expectations and add one of your own:

   - ☐ to discover God's call for my life
   - ☐ to discover the gifts God has given me
   - ☐ to discover how I can use those gifts in relationship to my call
   - ☐ to get to know some people who are willing to be open and honest about their struggles with God's call in their lives
   - ☐ to relax and have fun—and forget about God's call for awhile
   - ☐ to tackle some of the tougher issues in life—like my work and how I view money
   - ☐ to understand my attitude toward work
   - ☐ to develop a servant mind (like Christ's) in my work
   - ☐ to have a sense of community within our small group
   - ☐ to allow Scripture to challenge the way I think about my job, my calling, and my gifts
   - ☐ to recognize God's plan for my life
   - ☐ other: _____

**GROUND RULES**

3. If you are going to commit the next six weeks or sessions to this group, what are some things you want understood by the group before you commit? Check two or three, and add any of your own:

   - ☐ **Attendance**: to take the group seriously, and to give the meetings priority.
   - ☐ **Confidentiality**: anything that is said in the meetings will not be repeated outside the group.
   - ☐ **Accountability**: the group has the right to hold any member accountable for goals that member sets for himself/herself.
   - ☐ **Responsibility**: every group member accepts responsibility for the care and encouragement of the other group members.
   - ☐ **Openness**: the group is open to any person that is willing to accept the ground rules.
   - ☐ **Duration**: the group will commit to six more sessions. After this, the group will evaluate and recommit to another period if they wish to do so.

**SHARING**

Take a few minutes to share prayer requests with other group members. Go around and answer this question first:

*"How can we help you in prayer this week?"*

**PRAYER**

Take a moment to pray together. If you have not prayed out loud before, finish the sentence:

*"Hello, God, this is... (first name). I want to thank you for..."*

**ACTION**

1. Having this brief overview of what it means to be called of God, write down two or three concerns you have about your work, and the meaning you want to find from it. Refer to these during the next six weeks, and pray that you will discover answers to your concerns.

**2.** Pass around your books and have everyone sign the GROUP DIRECTORY inside the front cover.

**3.** Ask someone to bring refreshments next week.

**4.** Encourage the group to invite a friend to the group next week—to fill the "empty chair" (see page 2).

**Summary**... In two separate passages, Jesus calls his disciples from their previous line of work, and they immediately follow him. First this happens with Simon Peter, Andrew, James, and John (who were fishermen); then it happens with Matthew (who was a tax collector).

v. 18 **Sea of Galilee**... This freshwater sea (in the northern part of Palestine) was a focal point for much of Jesus' ministry. The northern end of the sea was particularly rich in fish. The ancient historian Josephus said that during the first century, more than 330 fishing boats operated on this sea. **Simon, called Peter**... Simon was the Greek form of the Hebrew name Simeon. Matthew 16:18 says that he actually received the name "Peter" later when he confessed that Jesus was the Christ. Jesus designated him as the "rock" ("Peter" meant "rock") on which Jesus would build his church. **casting a net**... This was probably a circular net with weights and a draw rope around its edge.

v. 19 **follow me**... Literally: "be my disciple." In those days, it was understood that rabbinical discipleship demanded intimate daily contact. It was not a part-time venture. In asking them to "follow" him, he was inviting them to join his band of disciples. Simon and Andrew would have been familiar with rabbis (who had small groups of students), as well as wandering Greek philosophers (who had disciples). **fishers of men**... In rabbinic and Greek literature, to "catch men" usually has an evil sense (see Jer. 16:16–18). But Jesus turned this meaning around. In telling them he would make them "fishers of men," he defined their task by using a metaphor which they would understand: they would be seeking converts to his teaching.

v. 20 **At once they left**... According to 4:12–17, Jesus had been living and preaching in Capernaum. These fishermen probably heard his message prior to their call. Still, they acted with great faith and courage. In the first century you lived where you were born, you stayed in your family cluster, and you took up your father's occupation.

v. 9 **Matthew**... Mark and Luke report that his name originally was "Levi." As a tax collector, Matthew would have been hated by both the religious establishment and the common people. **tax collector's booth**... Tax collectors in Galilee were Jews who were seen as traitors. They collaborated with the Roman power in order to become wealthy. Since only the tax collector knew the tax rate required by Rome, he was free to charge whatever the market would bear. Once he paid what he owed Rome, he kept the rest. A major international road ran through Capernaum. Possibly Matthew's job was to collect the tolls from the caravans that used the road, or he might have collected duties on goods shipped across the lake. **Follow me**... This is the key phrase regarding discipleship. Only those who leave their past behind to follow Jesus in faith and obedience are his disciples.

## SESSION 2

# Hearing God's Call

**PURPOSE:** To examine the issue of hearing God's call.

**AGENDA:** 🥣 Gathering 📖 Bible Study ♡ Caring Time

## GATHERING / 10 Minutes / All Together

*Leader: The purpose of the Gathering Time in this session is to help people get to know each other a bit better and share something personal about themselves. We encourage you to be the first one to share with the group.*

**OPEN**

**Step One: LIKE MUSIC TO MY EARS.** In each of the following pairs, which sound is more likely to be "music to your ears"?

- ❏ the crackling of a camp fire ❏ the sounds of city traffic at night
- ❏ the cry of "play ball!" ❏ waves crashing against the shore
- ❏ the laughter of children ❏ the laughter of an adult party
- ❏ a train whistle in the distance ❏ the bell of an ice cream truck
- ❏ the ring of the telephone ❏ the ring of a cash register
- ❏ the gurgling of a mtn. stream ❏ the talk of an opening-night crowd
- ❏ the purr of a kitten ❏ the hum of a well-tuned engine
- ❏ the silence of new-fallen snow ❏ the cheering of a crowd
- ❏ the sound of gentle rain ❏ the rapid talk of an auctioneer
- ❏ the chirping of a bird ❏ the crackling of a thunderstorm

**INTRODUCTION**

**Step Two: HEARING GOD'S CALL.** The things we want to hear are often easy to hear—like the things we have just talked about. But there are other times when we long to hear something clearly, and it is much more difficult. Such is the case with hearing God's call. We long for God's direction in life, but find it hard to hear what God is saying to us. This is complicated by the fact that some people (who claim to be following God's direction) do crazy and even violent things. People like David Koresh and Jim Jones make us wary of what it means to hear the voice of God calling us.

However, our lives cannot be guided by pathological aberrations. Too many people have served God and humanity because they heard God's call—people like Martin Luther King Jr. and Mother Teresa. There are also many ordinary, less publicized people. These include hospital volunteers, school aides, children's coaches, and others who have consistently made a difference in this world.

The question then becomes: how do we hear God's call? How can we differentiate between the voice of God, our own will, and all the other voices which call us in this world? Do we listen for an audible voice? Or do we need to pay attention to more subtle things around us and within us? James Fowler (who specializes in adult faith development) wrote a book entitled *Becoming Adult, Becoming Christian*. Fowler says that we should look for our vocation by "an approach that combines giving attention to one's gifts and inclinations, with a careful listening to the Christian story and vision, both in dynamic relation to the structure of needs and opportunities presented by the surrounding world."

**LEADER: Choose the Track One Bible study (below) or the Track Two study (page 15).**

In this session, we will look at this issue of hearing God's call. We will consider the factors mentioned by Fowler: our gifts (explored more fully in the next session), the Christian vision, and the needs of our world which call out for a response. In the Track One study, we will look at a story from Acts—how Paul was planning to go one way, but was called by God in another direction. We will talk about how he discerned that call, and what it means for us to discern God's call. In the Track Two study (from Paul's first letter to the Corinthians), we will consider the difference between what the world calls us to and what God calls us to.

# BIBLE STUDY / 30 Minutes / Groups of 4

*Leader: If you have more than 7 in this session, we recommend groups of 4—but not the same foursomes as last week. Ask one person in each foursome to be the Convener and complete the Bible study in the time allowed. Remember, you have two options for Bible Study: Track One and Track Two. Then regather for the Caring Time, allowing 20 minutes.*

# Called in a New Direction
## Acts 16:6–10

**STUDY**

This story occurred when the Apostle Paul was on a missionary journey to establish new churches. Prior to this, all of the churches he had established had been in the area known as Asia Minor. This call led to the first churches in Europe. Read Acts 16:6–10, and discuss the questions which follow with your group. Consult the Reference Notes on page 18 if you have difficulty with any words or phrases.

> **[6] Paul and his companions traveled throughout the region of Phrygia and Galatia, having been kept by the Holy Spirit from preaching the word in the province of Asia. [7] When they came to the border of Mysia, they tried to enter Bithynia, but the Spirit of Jesus would not allow them to. [8] So they passed by Mysia and went down to Troas. [9] During the night Paul had a vision of a man of Macedonia standing and begging him, "Come over to Macedonia and help us." [10] After Paul had seen the vision, we got ready at once to leave for Macedonia, concluding that God had called us to preach the gospel to them.**

*Acts 16:6–10, NIV*

1. From this passage, describe how Paul makes his decisions:
   - ❐ based on impulse and emotion
   - ❐ in a mystical, almost superstitious manner
   - ❐ in a manner that is sensitive to the needs of the moment
   - ❐ in a way that is constantly open to God's guidance

2. Choose one phrase from each line which best describes how you make decisions:
   - ❐ after much careful study ❐ according to my initial study
   - ❐ all is planned ahead ❐ based on present needs
   - ❐ after consulting others ❐ based on my own perceptions
   - ❐ with confidence I am right ❐ with a lot of uncertainty
   - ❐ with belief in God's guidance ❐ with a belief in my own judgment

3. In verse 7, "the Spirit of Jesus would not allow them" to enter Bithynia. What do you think that means?
   - ❐ they were physically restrained
   - ❐ they ran into difficulties, which they interpreted as Jesus not wanting them to go
   - ❐ Jesus verbally spoke to Paul and told him not to go
   - ❐ Paul just had a sense that this was not what Jesus wanted

4. If you had a dream like Paul's, how would you react to it?
   - ❐ I'd figure it was something I ate
   - ❐ I'd think it was my own subconscious desire to vacation in Greece
   - ❐ I wouldn't think twice about it
   - ❐ I would conclude what Paul concluded—this was where Jesus wanted me to go
   - ❐ I would never have such a dream

5. What do you think was the most influential factor in Paul's conclusion that Jesus wanted this change of direction for his ministry?
   - ❐ running into difficulties trying to go to Bithynia
   - ❐ the vision of the man in Macedonia
   - ❐ Paul's subconscious desire to expand his ministry in new areas
   - ❐ Paul's sensitivity to the needs of the moment

6. How sure do you think Paul was that this was the right way to go?
   - ❐ not at all sure—he was just guessing
   - ❐ rather unsure, but willing to take a chance
   - ❐ confident, but realizing he could be wrong
   - ❐ fully confident, knowing this was the right thing to do

7. When was the last time you made a decision that changed the direction of your life or work?
   - ❐ when I broke off my engagement to someone
   - ❐ when I changed majors in college
   - ❐ when I changed jobs
   - ❐ when I got divorced
   - ❐ when I made my commitment to Christ
   - ❐ other: _____

**8.** How confident were you at the time that the decision you talked about in question #7 was the right one?
- ☐ not at all sure
- ☐ rather unsure, but willing to take a chance
- ☐ confident, but realizing I could be wrong
- ☐ fully confident, knowing this was the right thing to do

**9.** What dream or vision for your future is calling you at this point in your life?

**10.** What will you look for as you seek to determine if this dream is God's call for your life?
- ☐ if I have a vision in the night (like Paul had at Troas)
- ☐ whether there are any barriers put in my way (like at Bithynia)
- ☐ God has to talk to me directly
- ☐ what is required by the needs of people around me (like the Macedonian)
- ☐ consistency with the values and teachings of Scripture
- ☐ other: _____

**LEADER: When you have completed the Bible study, move on to the Caring Time (page 17).**

# Called to a New Life
## 1 Corinthians 1:26–31

**STUDY** | The following passage is from the beginning of Paul's first letter to the church at Corinth. In it, he tries to help his readers understand the difference between what human wisdom says is good, and the life to which God calls us. Read 1 Corinthians 1:26–31 and answer the questions which follow with your group. Read the Reference Notes on pages 18–19 to help you understand the passage more fully.

> *²⁶ Brothers, think of what you were when you were called. Not many of you were wise by human standards; not many were influential; not many were of noble birth. ²⁷ But God chose the foolish things of the world to shame the wise; God chose the weak things of the world to shame the strong. ²⁸ He chose the lowly things of this world and the despised things—and the things that are not—to nullify the things that are, ²⁹ so that no one may boast before him. ³⁰ It is because of him that you are in Christ Jesus, who has become for us wisdom from God—that is, our righteousness, holiness and redemption. ³¹ Therefore, as it is written: "Let him who boasts boast in the Lord."*
>
> *1 Corinthians 1:26–31, NIV*

**1.** From this passage, how would you describe the Corinthian Christians to whom Paul was writing?
- ☐ a bunch of losers
- ☐ humble, common folk
- ☐ boastful
- ☐ working-class people
- ☐ people with many weaknesses
- ☐ other: _____

**2.** Why does Paul remind these Christians of their previous status?
- ❒ to shame them
- ❒ to keep them humble
- ❒ to remind them of their reliance on Christ for personal worth
- ❒ to show them what God can do with ordinary people

**3.** What is the significance of the fact that God "chose the foolish things of the world to shame the wise," and "the weak things of the world to shame the strong"?
- ❒ God is against people who are too independent and powerful
- ❒ what the world calls strength and wisdom is not always strength and wisdom
- ❒ to hear God's call, you have to tune out the values of the world
- ❒ the weakest person with God is stronger than the most powerful person without God
- ❒ God can use everyone in a great way
- ❒ so people couldn't boast before God

Use the following questions to compare the Corinthians' origins with your own:

**"Of noble birth":**

**4.** Finish this sentence: I was born...
- ❒ with a silver spoon in my mouth
- ❒ well, it was more like a tin cup
- ❒ with the advantage of a poor but loving family
- ❒ as an accident to those who did not want me
- ❒ to a typical middle-class family

**5.** Share where your ancestors were from, and the most unusual thing about your family tree.

**"Wisdom by human standards":**

**6.** Briefly describe your favorite year in school.

**7.** My experience with formal education was mostly:
- ❒ a disaster    ❒ wasted
- ❒ not what it could have been    ❒ positive
- ❒ essential to what I have achieved

**8.** In comparing myself to the Corinthians, I would have:
- ❒ fit right in
- ❒ been a little more educated
- ❒ been more educated, but maybe shamed by their "foolishness"
- ❒ other: _____

**"Influence":**

**9.** Where have you usually had the greatest amount of influence?
- ❒ in my job    ❒ in my church
- ❒ in the community    ❒ in our family
- ❒ in my dreams!    ❒ other: _____

**10.** Having read this passage, what quality of yours (that you have previously seen as "weak" or "foolish") do you now think God might be able to use?

**11.** Briefly describe a situation where God uses the weak, lowly, and despised to build his kingdom in our day.

**12.** What is the lesson of this passage for you?
- ☐ though others may see me as without potential, God knows better
- ☐ to hear God's call, I may have to disregard some of what the world says
- ☐ God can even use my weakness
- ☐ I may need more humility about my worldly accomplishments to truly be used by God
- ☐ other: _____

**LEADER:** When you have completed the Bible study, move on to the Caring Time (below).

**COMMENT**

The fact that the Corinthians can boast of party slogans is a clear indication that they overvalue human wisdom, and that they misunderstand the nature of the gospel. In this light, Paul explains in verses 18–25 the difference between human and divine wisdom. He shows that the gospel is decidedly not a type of human philosophy, because it involves such a reversal of human expectation. Who would have thought that God would work through the scandal of the cross? Only God could demonstrate his power through a dying, powerless "criminal."

Paul then goes on to "prove" that God does indeed work through weakness. He first looks at the Corinthians (verses 26–31), and then at himself (2:1–5). He points out that they were not very clever and he was not very persuasive. So the fact that they are Christians "proves" that God works through weakness. How else could the fact of the church of Corinth be explained?

# CARING TIME / 20 Minutes / All Together

*Leader: The purpose of the Caring Time in this session is to spend time in caring support for each other through Sharing, Prayer, and Action.*

**SHARING**

Take some time to share any personal prayer requests by answering the question:

*"How can we help you in prayer this week?"*

Think especially of areas of your life where you need God's direction.

**PRAYER**

Close with a short time of prayer, remembering the requests that were shared. If you choose to pray in silence, say the word "Amen" when you finish your prayer, so that the next person will know when to start.

**ACTION**

For a week, keep a list of every time someone puts down your ability (or the ability of someone around you). As you review this list, ask yourself the question: "How can God use what others see as a weakness in me?"

**REFERENCE NOTES:
ACTS 16:6–10**

**Summary**... In his missionary journey, the Apostle Paul is kept from going into Bithynia. Instead he is called to Macedonia in Greece, by the action of the Holy Spirit.

vv. 6–8  These verses represent a trip of some 250 miles, during which we are only told what Paul was *not* able to do. **Phrygia. . . Galatia. . . Asia**... These were all Roman provinces in the region known as Asia Minor. When Pliny wrote as governor in 112 AD, Christianity was already widespread in these areas. **the Holy Spirit. . . the Spirit of Jesus**... Luke clearly identifies the ongoing work of Jesus with the agency of the Holy Spirit in the lives of the apostles. **would not allow them to**... *Why* Jesus would not allow Paul and Silas to preach in Asia and Bithyna is not given. Later on, the apostle Peter was in contact with churches in that area so they were not deprived of the gospel (1 Pet. 1:1). *How* Jesus prevented them is also not explained. It may have been through a dream (v. 9) or a prophetic saying by one of Paul's companions (21:11). **Troas**... An important seaport on the Aegean Sea. While it appears Paul did not do any evangelistic work here at this time, he did later on (2 Cor. 2:12).

vv. 9–10  While in Troas, Paul had a vision that finally gave him a sense of where the Lord wanted him to go next. **Macedonia**... This area of northern Greece had been the dominant power under Alexander the Great in the 4th century BC. **we got ready**... The use of "we" here indicates the writer, Luke, was now with Paul. This is the first use of this pronoun in the book. Luke may have been a resident of this area.

**REFERENCE NOTES:
1 CORINTHIANS
1:26–31**

**Summary**... Paul discussed the difference between human and divine wisdom, because there were apparently people in Corinth who opposed Paul (and backed up their position with secular philosophy). Paul tells his readers that few of them were wise, influential, or of noble birth when they were called of God. Yet God used them in a way that puts to shame those who have those human qualities.

v. 26  **think of what you were**... In fact, in their own calling one sees this same paradox: the all-powerful God using "the weak things of the world." **not many**... The early church had special appeal to the poor and to those with little social standing. This was part of its offensiveness to the culture in general. The "wrong" people were attracted to it. On the other hand, it is clear that there were some influential people in the Corinthian Church. For example, there was Crispus, a former head of the synagogue who had a position of status in the Jewish community (Ac. 18:8). And there was Erastus, who as director of public works in Corinth, was a man of wealth and power (Rom. 16:23). **wise**... This refers to people with education or philosophical training. **influential**... This means people in high positions (politically or socially). **noble birth**... These were people of distinguished families who may have held Roman citizenship. The church at Corinth was not unique in the fact that it was made up primarily of the lower classes of society. In 178 AD, Celsus put down Christianity, saying that they seemed to proclaim: "Let no cultured person draw near, none wise, none sensible; for all that kind of thing we count evil; but if any man is ignorant, if any is wanting in sense and culture, if any is a fool let him come boldly." But it was the strength of Christianity that the vast numbers (cast out by the cultured society) found a home and a sense of purpose in Christian faith.

v. 27 **The foolish things**... These are the people who, in the estimation of the people described in verse 26, were insignificant. **to shame**... The calling of the insignificant shows that the opinions of the "wise" (about the worth of certain people or about how one approached God) were wrong.

v. 28 **lowly**... the opposite of "noble birth" in verse 26. **The things that are not/ the things that are**... God chooses the "nobodies," and thus exposes the foolishness of the way the world defines the "somebodies."

v. 29 **boast**... A church composed of such people ought to know that they were not chosen based on who they were or what they had done. To boast is to wrongly evaluate one's own gifts, to put confidence in them, and to express this with a tinge of pride. To boast in this context is to place one's confidence before God in one's own accomplishments, an attitude which is totally antithetical to the gospel of grace.

v. 30 **wisdom from God**... In Proverb and Ecclesiastes, Wisdom was personi-fied and hailed as a reliable guide to life. Paul indicates that Jesus Christ really is Wisdom made flesh. For Paul, "wisdom" is not found in the speculations of the human mind, but in the action of God in Christ. **Righteousness, holiness, and redemption**... These are three of Paul's metaphors for salvation. **righteousness**... Christ took upon himself the guilt of human sin. His righteousness assures them of acquittal. **holiness**... People cannot come before a holy God because they are not morally pure. But Christ provides what people lack. His holiness suffices for them, and so a relationship with God is assured. **redemption**... This has the sense of "deliverance." On the cross, Christ freed humanity from its bondage to sin.

## SESSION 3

# Finding Your Gift

**PURPOSE:** To discover how to find our gifts and abilities.

**AGENDA:**  Gathering [ ] Bible Study [♡] Caring Time

## GATHERING / 10 Minutes / All Together

*Leader: Read the instructions for Step One and set the pace by going first. Then read the Introduction in Step Two and move on to the Bible study.*

**OPEN**

**Step One: CHILD PRODIGIES.** For each of the categories below, pick someone from your group who you think might have been a "child prodigy" (excelling in that area). Assign everyone in the group to at least one of the categories. Then each person should share how accurate the group's judgment was regarding their childhood experience.

_____ smuggling stray animals into the house
_____ having (and surviving) childhood accidents
_____ making up imaginative excuses for misbehavior
_____ talking at an early age
_____ climbing the highest trees in the neighborhood
_____ having the most successful lemonade stand
_____ watching horror movies without having nightmares
_____ inventing games that the other children wanted to play
_____ going through the most new clothes in a year
_____ taking the car on a joy ride at an early age
_____ streaking in public
_____ embarrassing their parents in public

**INTRODUCTION**

**Step Two: FINDING YOUR GIFT.** Integrally related to hearing God's call is finding your gift. Once we know what talents or abilities God has given us, then we have a big clue as to what God is calling us to do. Richard Nelson Bolles is the author of the bestselling book on job-hunting, *What Color is Your Parachute?*. Bolles says that our enthusiasm for doing something, and for using the gift (or gifts) we have been given, are important aspects in discovering our "call" and "mission." We don't need more people in the world drawing a paycheck and living for the weekend. Instead, "what the world does need is more people who feel true enthusiasm for their work. People who have taken the time to *think*—that is, to think out what they uniquely can do, and what they uniquely have to offer the world."

**LEADER: Choose the Track One Bible study (below) or the Track Two study (page 23).**

Bolles also says that skills can be divided into three general categories: working with data or information, working with people, or working with things. The first step in finding our gift is to find which of those categories we work with best. Another step is going to a vocational counselor. We can also talk to friends about the strengths they see in us. And, through the process of trial and error, we can discover which tasks we do best.

In this session, we will look at how we find our gifts. In the Track One study (from the book of Acts), we will look at some men who were selected to minister to the needs of others on the basis of their gifts. In the Track Two study (from Paul's first letter to the Corinthians), we will look at Paul's assurance that we are all given gifts by the Spirit for the common good, and that these work together like parts of a body.

# BIBLE STUDY / 30 Minutes / Groups of 4

*Leader: A quick reminder that if you have more than 7 in this session, have the group split into groups of 4. It's good not to have the same foursomes as last week. After the Bible study, ask each Convener to bring their group back to your central meeting place for the Caring Time.*

## A Division of Duties
## Acts 6:1–7

**STUDY**

The following passage relates an incident that occurred shortly after the Church was born. It shows how growth in this infant church went hand-in-hand with giving responsibility to people with different gifts. Read Acts 6:1–7 and answer the questions which follow with your group. If you have questions about difficult words or phrases, consult the Reference Notes on pages 27–28.

**6** *In those days when the number of disciples was increasing, the Grecian Jews among them complained against the Hebraic Jews because their widows were being overlooked in the daily distribution of food. ² So the Twelve gathered all the disciples together and said, "It would not be right for us to neglect the ministry of the word of God in order to wait on tables. ³ Brothers, choose seven men from among you who are known to be full of the Spirit and wisdom. We will turn this responsibility over to them ⁴ and will give our attention to prayer and the ministry of the word."*
*⁵ This proposal pleased the whole group. They chose Stephen, a man full of faith and of the Holy Spirit; also Philip, Procorus, Nicanor, Timon, Parmenas, and Nicolas from Antioch, a convert to Judaism. ⁶ They presented these men to the apostles, who prayed and laid their hands on them.*
*⁷ So the word of God spread. The number of disciples in Jerusalem increased rapidly, and a large number of priests became obedient to the faith.*

*Acts 6:1–7, NIV*

1. From this snapshot, choose three of the following which describe the Christian community in Jerusalem at this time:
   ❑ diverse                    ❑ good at conflict-management
   ❑ well-organized             ❑ exciting
   ❑ cooperative                ❑ confrontational
   ❑ honest                     ❑ dynamic
   ❑ Spirit-filled              ❑ spiritual

2. If you were one of the Twelve and heard this complaint by the Grecian Jews, what would have been your first response?
   ❑ sounds like little kids—"she's getting more than I am!"
   ❑ what do they expect from us—we're doing so much already
   ❑ I'm glad they felt comfortable telling us about this
   ❑ you have to expect conflict—when you are growing fast
   ❑ if people are in need, we must respond quickly

3. In verse 2, the Twelve said: "it would not be right for us to neglect the ministry of the word of God in order to wait on tables..." How do you respond to their statement?
   ❑ it sounds like they were too good for that
   ❑ they were so excited about what they were doing, they didn't want to interrupt it
   ❑ they realized the number of things that needed to be done were more than they could handle without additional help
   ❑ other: _____

*"Work is love made visible. And if you cannot work with love, but only with distaste, it is better that you should leave your work and sit at the gate of the temple and take alms of those who work with joy."*
*—Kahlil Gibran*

4. Place an "X" on the line below to indicate which of the two statements you agree with more:

   **All gifts are of equal value and dignity** _____ **Some gifts have greater value and dignity than others**

5. Which responsibility at home (or work) would you gladly give up? Never give up?

6. How do you think Stephen and the others felt when they were selected for this task?
   ❑ honored—especially after the apostles prayed for them
   ❑ imposed upon—another "committee" assignment
   ❑ insulted—to have to do the dirty work others didn't want to do
   ❑ angry—that they were the ones who were chosen

7. If you helped to select someone for this task, what qualities or skills would you look for? (Choose the top two.)
   ❑ anyone who would do it
   ❑ tact and diplomacy—to deal with the two factions
   ❑ good listeners—widows need someone to talk to
   ❑ dietary knowledge
   ❑ patience—to deal with the elderly
   ❑ "full of the Spirit and wisdom"—like Acts says
   ❑ humility and a spirit of service
   ❑ other: _____

**8.** What is the significance of the fact that these men were chosen—rather than volunteered—for the job?
- ❏ it shows that the early church was autocratic
- ❏ others often recognize our gifts more easily than we do
- ❏ probably no one would have volunteered for such a job
- ❏ volunteers may not have been suited to the job

**9.** What job or task have you been especially selected to do where you were proud of being selected? (It can be at work, at church, or in your community.) What gifts were required of you to do this task?

**10.** What job or task have you been asked to do where you were embarrassed about being selected? (It can be at work, at church, or in your home.) After studying this passage, do you feel differently about that task?
- ❏ yes—I can see where I was used by God even in that menial task
- ❏ maybe—but the task was still menial
- ❏ no—the task was beneath anyone
- ❏ no—and I don't want to view that horrible task any differently
- ❏ other: _____

**LEADER: When you have completed the Bible study, move on to the Caring Time (page 27).**

**11.** Which of the categories of skills that Richard Nelson Bolles mentioned (in the Introduction) do you work best with?
- ❏ data or information
- ❏ people
- ❏ things

# A Variety of Gifts
## 1 Corinthians 12:7–27

**STUDY**

Paul wrote the following passage because some Christians at Corinth apparently felt that everyone should be the same and have the same gift. This attitude was causing division in the church. So Paul wrote to tell them that no gifts are inferior and that all are necessary. Read 1 Corinthians 12:7–27 and discuss the questions which follow with your group. If you need help with a difficult word or phrase, check the Reference Notes on pages 28–29.

*[7] Now to each one the manifestation of the Spirit is given for the common good. [8] To one there is given through the Spirit the message of wisdom, to another the message of knowledge by means of the same Spirit, [9] to another faith by the same Spirit, to another gifts of healing by that one Spirit, [10] to another miraculous powers, to another prophecy, to another distinguishing between spirits, to another speaking in different kinds of tongues, and to still another the interpretation of tongues. [11] All these are the work of one and the same Spirit, and he gives them to each one, just as he determines.*

*[12] The body is a unit, though it is made up of many parts; and though all its parts are many, they form one body. So it is with Christ. [13] For we were all baptized by one Spirit into one body—whether Jews or Greeks, slave or free—and we were all given the one Spirit to drink.*

*14 Now the body is not made up of one part but of many. 15 If the foot should say, "Because I am not a hand, I do not belong to the body," it would not for that reason cease to be part of the body. 16 And if the ear should say, "Because I am not an eye, I do not belong to the body," it would not for that reason cease to be part of the body. 17 If the whole body were an eye, where would the sense of hearing be? If the whole body were an ear, where would the sense of smell be? 18 But in fact God has arranged the parts in the body, every one of them, just as he wanted them to be. 19 If they were all one part, where would the body be? 20 As it is, there are many parts, but one body.*

*21 The eye cannot say to the hand, "I don't need you!" And the head cannot say to the feet, "I don't need you!" 22 On the contrary, those parts of the body that seem to be weaker are indispensable, 23 and the parts that we think are less honorable we treat with special honor. And the parts that are unpresentable are treated with special modesty, 24 while our presentable parts need no special treatment. But God has combined the members of the body and has given greater honor to the parts that lacked it, 25 so that there should be no division in the body, but that its parts should have equal concern for each other. 26 If one part suffers, every part suffers with it; if one part is honored, every part rejoices with it.*

*27 Now you are the body of Christ, and each one of you is a part of it.*

*1 Corinthians 12:7–27, NIV*

1. If you were in the church at Corinth the day Paul's letter was read, what would be your first impression?
   ❒ yeah, sure, Paul—all our gifts are equal
   ❒ you have got to be kidding
   ❒ evidently Paul doesn't realize the importance of my gifts
   ❒ I'm sorry, Paul—I can't believe my measly gift is of any real value
   ❒ I sure would like to believe you, Paul
   ❒ would you mind telling that to so-and-so?

2. What attitudes toward spiritual gifts dominate in your church (regardless of your church's official doctrinal position)? Spiritual gifts are for:
   ❒ pastors only                    ❒ all believers
   ❒ the good of others              ❒ the first-century church only
   ❒ the more spiritually mature  ❒ other: _____
   ❒ believers who have had a post-conversion experience

3. Which of the implications of Paul's body image do you think needs to be taken more seriously by the church today?
   ❒ the body is a single unit—v. 12
   ❒ yet it is made up of various parts—v. 12
   ❒ the different parts do not have the freedom to opt out of the body—vv. 14–16
   ❒ each part, though quite different, is necessary—vv. 17–19
   ❒ each part is vital and needed—vv. 21–22
   ❒ different parts have different functions and are presented in different ways—vv. 22–25
   ❒ if one part of the body suffers, the whole body suffers—v. 26
   ❒ the church is like a body—v. 27
   ❒ it has many parts to it (as represented by the different gifts given to different members)

"Sick or well, blind or seeing, bond or free, we are here for a purpose, and however we are situated, we please God better with useful deeds than with many prayers of pious resignation."
—Helen Keller

4. When have you felt like you were part of a unit, where all the parts worked together for a common goal?
   - ❒ on a sports team
   - ❒ at work
   - ❒ in a political campaign
   - ❒ never
   - ❒ in a sorority/fraternity
   - ❒ on a church project
   - ❒ on a community project
   - ❒ in the armed services

5. Below are a list of characteristics of a church which was organized around spiritual gifts. Choose three of the characteristics you would most enjoy in that type of church:
   - ❒ we would not have the same few people doing all the jobs, but rather many people doing specific jobs
   - ❒ people would enjoy what they are doing, since by definition one enjoys using a gift
   - ❒ our ministry would be more effective, since people would be skilled at their jobs and successful in the exercise of their gifts
   - ❒ people would probably give more time to the church, since they would love what they do
   - ❒ we would make an impact on our community, since it would both see and experience our ministry
   - ❒ we would not have to worry about finding people each year to do all the jobs
   - ❒ our minister would be freed up to train us to use our gifts better
   - ❒ we would have more direct experience of the Holy Spirit

*"The community of faith, at its best, is an 'ecology of vocations.'"*
*—James Fowler*

6. What obstacles keep you from sharing your gifts with the church?
   - ❒ I'm too scared
   - ❒ I'm too embarrassed
   - ❒ I really don't think my gift is useful
   - ❒ I'm not sure I have a gift
   - ❒ I'm too jealous of someone else's gift
   - ❒ spiritual pride—I really think my gifts are superior

7. If you could pass out awards to people who have contributed their spiritual gifts to your life as part of the body of Christ, who would you nominate for special recognition in these categories?
   - _____ **APOSTLE:** one who planted the message of Christ in me
   - _____ **PROPHET:** one who proclaimed the message of Christ faithfully
   - _____ **TEACHER:** one who instructed and established me in the faith
   - _____ **WORKER OF MIRACLES:** one who believed God for great things
   - _____ **GIFTS OF HEALING:** one who was there for me when I was hurting
   - _____ **GIFTS OF ADMINISTRATION:** one who helped me discipline my life

8. What does the Church need to do better to be this kind of unit where everyone knows they have a part?
   - ❒ rely more on the Spirit
   - ❒ be more accepting of diversity
   - ❒ be more aware of the gifts people have
   - ❒ provide more training so people can develop their gifts

9. To carry out the Church's mission to "suffer with those who suffer and rejoice with those who are honored," which of the following does the Church need most?

☐ more "ears"—to listen to people who are hurting
☐ more "eyes"—to observe the needs around us
☐ more "arms"—to reach out and hold each other
☐ more "hands"—to pitch in and help each other with our tasks
☐ more "legs"—to put our good thoughts into action
☐ more "heads"—to organize our efforts to care

10. Which of the tasks listed in question #9 do you do best?

11. Use the scale below to measure to what degree you feel your gifts are needed in each of the following contexts:

| 1 | 2 | 3 | 4 | 5 | 6 | 7 | 8 | 9 | 10 |
|---|---|---|---|---|---|---|---|---|---|
| not needed | | | needed, but replaceable | | | | essential, irreplaceable | | |

___ at home
___ at work
___ at church
___ in my community

**COMMENT**

Paul continues to teach about spiritual gifts. We listen to his words with a great fascination. For many of us, this is a whole new world. The gift of healing, the gift of miracles, the gift of prophecy—we may never have heard of these gifts before, much less experienced them. The more "supernatural" gifts tend to scare us.

This was not the case in Corinth. They had heard about and reveled in these gifts. They exercised these gifts constantly and prided themselves on them. In fact, they went overboard with these gifts. So Paul tries to slow them down. The gifts are authentic and from God. They are necessary for the church. But they have to be used in the right way. Clearly the Corinthians were using them in the wrong way.

We, of course, listen in fascination to all of this. Our problem is generally not an overexuberant use of spiritual gifts. Our problem is that we don't use spiritual gifts as much as we should. It is not that we do not manifest any spiritual gifts in our church. We do. For example, we know that certain people have the gift of teaching. Others are always helping people out. Still others like nothing better than to sort out the best way to run a particular program. It is just that we are often not aware that these are spiritual gifts. Therefore, we do not use these gifts to their full extent, because we haven't realized that this is the thing the Lord wants us to do in his church. Nor do we get training in the use of our gifts in order to expand our ministries.

**LEADER: When you have completed the Bible study, move on to the Caring Time (page 27).**

# CARING TIME / 20 Minutes / All Together

*Leader: Bring all the groups of 4 back together for a time of caring. Follow the three steps below.*

**SHARING**

One at a time, go around to each person in the group and ask the others to share what they see as his or her gifts.

**PRAYER**

Thank God for the gifts of the people in the group, and pray for God's guidance in using those gifts the way he wants us to.

**ACTION**

On a piece of paper, write the gifts the group members said they saw in you. Write each one at the top of a column. Then during the week, write down instances where you use that gift. At the end of the week, ask yourself: what does this say about the way I am using my gifts?

**REFERENCE NOTES:**
**ACTS 6:1–7**

**Summary**... A dispute arose between the Grecian Jews and the Hebraic Jews over how the widows of the Grecian Jews were treated in the distribution of food. The twelve Apostles settled it by appointing seven men to oversee this ministry. The dispute was resolved and the church continued to grow.

v. 1    The problem in the church centered around questions of fairness in the distribution of food to the poor widows in the church. Many elderly Jews (who had lived most of their lives elsewhere in the empire) came to live in Jerusalem for their final years. Those who were widowed, now far from home, were subject to poverty. It was these women who were being neglected. **Grecian Jews**... Jews who came from outside Palestine (and for whom Aramaic and Hebrew were relatively unknown languages). Their synagogue worship was also conducted in their native languages. **Hebraic Jews**... Native Palestinians who spoke Aramaic as their daily language. Since all the apostles were Hebraic Jews, they may have been more sensitive and aware of the needs of those with whom they could easily communicate. **daily distribution**... While there was no welfare system or pension plan for widows, Jewish culture had a strong tradition of caring for their widows (see especially Deut. 14:28–29). The early church continued this tradition, providing food for their widows.

v. 2    **the Twelve**... These were the original twelve disciples whom Jesus chose, with a man named Matthias selected to replace Judas (who had betrayed Christ and later killed himself—see Ac. 1:15–26). These men had special authority in the Church of this time. **wait on tables**... Lit. "to serve tables." This does not refer to being a waiter! At that time, banking was done by people sitting at a table. To "serve tables" was a figure of speech for handling financial transactions. The apostles recognized their inability to meet the increasing needs of the community on their own. The men who were chosen would assume full responsibility for the task of the distribution of the community's funds. While many churches use this passage as the basis for the office of deacon, no title is given to these men. However, the Greek verb "to serve" is the root word from which the English word "deacon" comes.

v. 3    **seven men**... It was common Jewish practice to appoint boards of seven men to deal with various responsibilities (Marshall). **full of the Spirit**... Whereas being "filled with the Spirit" appears to be a momentary endowment of power for witness (4:8, 31), "full of the Spirit" indicates an ongoing lifestyle that reflects the presence of Christ (Williams). **and wisdom**... Proven insight into difficult situations.

v. 5   **from Antioch, a convert to Judaism**... Note that a proselyte was included in this group. Luke stresses that he is from Antioch. The gospel would soon be taken to this city. And Antioch would become the "headquarters" for the upcoming Gentile missionary effort. The names of the men who were chosen strongly indicate that all seven were Greek-speaking Jews. Perhaps they also served as a bridge between the Palestinian apostles and the Greek-speaking Jews to help avoid further unintentional difficulties between the two groups. **Stephen**... This man moves to center stage in chapter 7 and later becomes one of the first martyrs. **Philip. . . and Nicholas**... Like Stephen, Philip demonstrated gifts of evangelism, not unlike those of the apostles (see v. 8; 8:4–8; 21:80). Little is known of these other people, but it is noteworthy that all of them have Greek names. This was a way to give Greek-speaking Jews some representation in the authority structure of the Church.

v. 6   **laid their hands on them**... In the OT, the laying on of hands signified either a blessing (Gen. 48:14) or a commissioning (Num. 27:18, 23) (Williams). In the NT period, the laying on of hands was observed in healing, blessing, ordaining or commissioning, and imparting spiritual gifts. The act signified that these Seven would now be the representatives of the apostles in the matter over which they were given responsibility.

v. 7   This is the final summary of the church that is limited to Jerusalem. From here on, the church continually expands beyond its place of origin. **priests**... Most priests lived outside of Jerusalem, serving in the Temple only two weeks out of every year. While the Sadducees controlled the priesthood, many of the priests, like Zechariah (the father of John the Baptist—see Lk. 1:6), were sincerely devout men.

**REFERENCE NOTES:**
**1 CORINTHIANS**
**12:7–27**

**Summary**... Paul assures us that the Spirit gives gifts to each person for the common good. Different people with different gifts work together like the different parts of a body. You can't have a true body if all the parts are the same. No part can say it doesn't need the other parts. That's the way it is in the Church, the body of Christ. "The body is a unit, though it is made up of many parts; and though all its parts are many, they form one body. So it is with Christ" (v. 12). This verse is the central point to this entire passage. The unity in the body exists because all were baptized into one Spirit, and all drink from one Spirit. Paul is not concerned with how people become believers. His concern is how believers overcome obstacles to become one body. Paul then points to the diversity of the Body of Christ: the one body has many different parts to it, and each gift is vital (regardless of its nature).

v. 7   **manifestation**... This is another way of saying a gift of the Spirit. These are given not for individual ego-building or profit, but for the common good and community growth.

v. 8   **wisdom/knowledge**... It is not clear how these gifts differ. It is possible that a *message of wisdom* focused on practical, ethical instruction, while a *message of knowledge* involved exposition of truth about God. **wisdom. . . knowledge. . . faith**... This is not intended as a complete list of gifts, but rather a sampling. Other gifts are listed in Romans 12:6–8.

v. 9 **faith**... This is a special ability "to claim from God extraordinary manifestations of power in the natural world" (Barrett). **healing**... This is the special ability to effect miraculous cures.

v. 10 **miraculous powers**... The gift of exorcism may be in view. **prophecy**... These are inspired utterances given in ordinary (not ecstatic) speech, distinguished from teaching and wisdom by its unpremeditated nature (see ch. 14). **distinguish between spirits**... Just because a person *claimed* to be inspired by the Holy Spirit did not make it true. Those who possessed this gift were able to determine whether such speech came from the Holy Spirit or not. **interpretation**... This gift allowed a person to understand and explain to others what was said by someone who spoke in tongues.

v. 11 Paul underscores his main point: the gifts are given by the Spirit's choice and for his purposes. Hence, they are not a sign of spiritual attainment.

v. 12 **So it is with Christ**... The Church is the body of Christ (v. 27), and so indeed Christ can be understood to be made up of many parts. Yet he is also the Lord (v. 3), and thus Head over the Church.

v. 13 **baptized by one Spirit**... The phrase should read, "baptized *in* one Spirit." Paul's concern is not with the means by which believers are baptized, but with the common reality of the Holy Spirit in which all believers exist (Fee). **Jews or Greeks, slave or free**... See Galatians 3:28.

vv. 15–26 Paul argues: It would be silly for one part of a person's body to decide not to belong to the body, because it was not like another part. If all Christians had the same gift, the body would be impoverished. In a similar manner, it would be ludicrous for Christians to opt out of the body of Christ (presumably by not using their gifts during worship), because they do not have the same gift as someone else. A Christian ought not to deny the value, need, or function of anyone's spiritual gift simply because it is different from their own.

vv. 21–22 Each part of the body *needs* the others. No single gift (e.g., tongues) can stand alone. Wholeness requires all the parts to function together. **weaker**... "The delicate organs, such as the eye; and the invisible organs such as the heart" (Barrett).

v. 27 Paul sums up the meaning of his metaphor. **the body of Christ**... Paul conveys the idea that Christ rules over this body, and that this body belongs to him.

# SESSION 4

# Taking the Risk

**PURPOSE:** To discover what it means to take creative risks in search of our call.

**AGENDA:**  Gathering  📖 Bible Study  ♡ Caring Time

## GATHERING / 10 Minutes / All Together

*Leader: Read the instructions for Step One and set the pace by going first. Then read the Introduction in Step Two and move on to the Bible study.*

**OPEN**

**Step One: FINAL JEOPARDY.** Imagine you are entering the final round of *Jeopardy!* with $4,000. Your opponents have $4,500 and $5,000. How much of your $4,000 are you going to risk if the final category is the following?

_____ understanding the opposite sex
_____ current rock groups
_____ Federal Income Tax forms
_____ auto mechanics
_____ popular video games
_____ names in the Old Testament
_____ soap opera couples
_____ politically correct language

**INTRODUCTION**

**Step Two: TAKING THE RISK.** In an ideal world, everyone would be absolutely sure what their calling was and what their gifts were. And everyone would know  that using those gifts in their calling would lead to success and satisfaction. However, this is not an ideal world. So when we are in one job (and strongly suspect that our true calling is in another area) we may have to risk switching jobs, even though we are not 100% sure. We might risk giving up a secure job with a steady income for an unsure one with less certain finances. A college student may risk angering parents (who want him or her to go into the field they have visualized) in order to hold out for his or her own vision (even though that vision may be uncertain). In the real world, finding and following our calling involves risk-taking.

To say that taking risks is necessary to find our calling in the real world is not to say that all such venturing is bad. Actually, having to risk can be part of life's excitement. Author Bruce Larson (in his book *There's a Lot More to Health than Not Being Sick*) writes what his physician told him when he reached middle age. "Middle age is a time when people are advised to take

30

it easy. You start to live very cautiously. You avoid anything new or risky and you end up hastening the whole aging process." Risk can add to the excitement of life. And that can actually make us healthier! Larson goes on to discuss God's role in this, writing: "I acknowledge that risk for risk's sake, while it may be healthier, is not very productive. But God seems to be calling us to a life of *creative* risk. We are to be those people who are prayerfully seeking to bring about God's will and way in the affairs of men and who can give themselves to those causes with abandon."

Creative risk—it is a vital ingredient in finding and living out our call. This session will help us to see what it means to risk as we search for that call. In Track One, we will look at the parable of the talents (Matthew 25:14–30). In it, we will consider how Jesus commended the servants who took some risks to invest in the kingdom. In Track Two, we will examine Paul's advice to young Timothy that he not approach life with timidity (2 Timothy 1:3–14).

## BIBLE STUDY / 30 Minutes / Groups of 4

*Leader: Help the groups decide on the Track One or Track Two Bible study. If there are more than 7 people, divide into groups of 4, and ask one person in each group to be the Convener. Finish the Bible study in 30 minutes, and gather the groups together for the Caring Time.*

# The Risk of Investment
# Matthew 25:14–30

**STUDY**

The following parable is one of many that Jesus told to clarify our role in doing the work of the kingdom of God. Read Matthew 25:14–30 and discuss the questions which follow with your group. If you have difficulty with a word or phrase, consult the Reference Notes on pages 37–38.

*[14] "Again, it will be like a man going on a journey, who called his servants and entrusted his property to them. [15] To one he gave five talents of money, to another two talents, and to another one talent, each according to his ability. Then he went on his journey. [16] The man who had received the five talents went at once and put his money to work and gained five more. [17] So also, the one with the two talents gained two more. [18] But the man who had received the one talent went off, dug a hole in the ground and hid his master's money.*

*[19] "After a long time the master of those servants returned and settled accounts with them. [20] The man who had received the five talents brought the other five. 'Master,' he said, 'you entrusted me with five talents. See, I have gained five more.'*

*[21] "His master replied, 'Well done, good and faithful servant! You have been faithful with a few things; I will put you in charge of many things. Come and share your master's happiness!'*

*[22] "The man with the two talents also came. 'Master,' he said, 'you entrusted me with two talents; see, I have gained two more.'*

*[23] "His master replied, 'Well done, good and faithful servant! You have been faithful with a few things; I will put you in charge of many things. Come and share your master's happiness!'*

**24** *"Then the man who had received the one talent came. 'Master,' he said, 'I knew that you are a hard man, harvesting where you have not sown and gathering where you have not scattered seed. **25** So I was afraid and went out and hid your talent in the ground. See, here is what belongs to you.'*

**26** *"His master replied, 'You wicked, lazy servant! So you knew that I harvest where I have not sown and gather where I have not scattered seed?* **27** *Well then, you should have put my money on deposit with the bankers, so that when I returned I would have received it back with interest.*

**28** *" 'Take the talent from him and give it to the one who has the ten talents.* **29** *For everyone who has will be given more, and he will have an abundance. Whoever does not have, even what he has will be taken from him.* **30** *And throw that worthless servant outside, into the darkness, where there will be weeping and gnashing of teeth.' "*

*Matthew 25:14–30, NIV*

1. Based on this parable, if Jesus were an investment counselor today, what kind of investment strategy do you think he might advise?
   - ❏ hide it under your mattress
   - ❏ passbook savings and low-risk investment
   - ❏ a conservative, balanced portfolio
   - ❏ a portfolio based on high-risk investment in "growth" stocks

2. In which of the following are you most likely to invest your money and time? Choose three and briefly explain why you chose them:
   - ❏ a passbook savings account
   - ❏ a certificate of deposit
   - ❏ stocks and bonds
   - ❏ other people
   - ❏ helping others
   - ❏ a political organization
   - ❏ environmental causes
   - ❏ your child's education
   - ❏ your marriage
   - ❏ a charitable organization
   - ❏ church/religious organization
   - ❏ your family
   - ❏ commodity futures market
   - ❏ a money market account
   - ❏ U.S. savings bonds
   - ❏ a life insurance policy
   - ❏ gold
   - ❏ other: _____

3. What did Jesus mean when he said, "For everyone who has will be given more, and he will have in abundance. Whoever does not have, even what he has will be taken away"?
   - ❏ "the rich get richer; the poor get poorer"
   - ❏ God favors those who are financially successful
   - ❏ when we use what we have been given for God and others, we get more
   - ❏ using gifts strengthens them; neglecting them allows them to atrophy

4. Who do you identify with in this parable?
   - ❏ the five-talent servant—God has given me so much
   - ❏ the two-talent servant—just an average person with average gifts and blessings
   - ❏ the one-talent servant—others seem to have so much more to give
   - ❏ the Master—my main gift is empowering others to use their gifts

*"...when we search for a sense of Mission we are searching for reassurance that the world is at least a little bit richer for our being here; and a little bit poorer after our going."*
*—Richard Nelson Bolles*

5. What kind of reward do the faithful servants receive from the master? Which of the possible rewards sound most appealing to you as you serve Jesus Christ?
   - ❏ a life of ease
   - ❏ friendship with the master
   - ❏ a new car
   - ❏ praise from the master
   - ❏ satisfaction of a job well done
   - ❏ a golden crown
   - ❏ early retirement
   - ❏ more responsibility
   - ❏ better food and lodging
   - ❏ other: _____

6. Which statement summarizes your parents' attitude toward your doing risky things as a child?
   - ❏ "Don't do anything where you might get hurt"
   - ❏ "Better not to try than to fail"
   - ❏ "Look before you leap"
   - ❏ "When you fall down, get back up and try again"
   - ❏ "The only real mistake is not trying"
   - ❏ "You can do whatever you set your mind on"

7. Which of the following risks did you take as a child or adolescent?
   - ❏ going out for "dangerous" sports
   - ❏ asking someone out when I wasn't sure he/she liked me
   - ❏ skipping school
   - ❏ driving crazily
   - ❏ working on a hazardous science project
   - ❏ climbing high trees and rock formations
   - ❏ trying out for exclusive groups (like cheerleader, concert choir)

8. How do you differentiate between healthy risk-taking and foolhardy risk-taking?

9. Write three of the talents which you have discovered or which others have said you have (from last session). Then assign each talent a number (from the scale) according to how well you're using that talent right now:

| 1 | 2 | 3 | 4 | 5 | 6 | 7 | 8 | 9 | 10 |
|---|---|---|---|---|---|---|---|---|---|
| **burying it** | | | | | | | | | **fully invested** |

10. Which of the following statements describes how you feel about the way you are currently "investing" your life?
    - ❏ I am quite satisfied
    - ❏ I would like to make some changes
    - ❏ I need to change, but don't know what to do
    - ❏ I don't know what it means to invest my life
    - ❏ I haven't done a very good job investing my life

11. What changes would be necessary to in order for you to be more satisfied with your life's investment?
    - ❏ get into a profession that more fully utilizes my talents
    - ❏ find ways to use my talents in a volunteer capacity
    - ❏ risk using some talents I have been afraid to use
    - ❏ stop worrying about failure and try *something*
    - ❏ I'm already investing my talents pretty well

**LEADER:** When you have completed the Bible study, move on to the Caring Time (page 36).

**12.** What is Jesus teaching you in this parable?
- ☐ that making money without working is important
- ☐ that investing in God's kingdom is very important
- ☐ that he has given Christians a "job" to do until he returns
- ☐ that we should invest our "talents" (abilities) in God's kingdom
- ☐ that judgment is coming for those who are unwilling to risk and do not invest their lives wisely

**COMMENT**

Jesus told a parable about three men who were entrusted with different amounts of money by their master. The first was given five talents, the second two talents, and the third one talent. The first two invested the money and doubled their investment. The third just buried it out of fear. The master commended the first two servants, but reprimanded the last. He said that he who has will be given more, but he who has not, even what he has will be taken away.

This parable (similar the one in Lk. 19:11–27) underscores three points: (1) Christ's kingdom will not be established at this time; (2) discipleship means faithful service to God while awaiting Christ's return, and (3) judgment awaits those who fail to invest themselves in the work of the kingdom.

# No More Timidity
## 2 Timothy 1:3–14

**STUDY**

The following passage was written to Timothy, a young Greek who Paul took under his wing. It is a personal word of encouragement to Timothy to be faithful. Read 2 Timothy 1:3–14, and discuss the questions which follow with your group. Take a look at the Reference Notes on pages 38–39 for a fuller understanding of the text.

*³ I thank God, whom I serve, as my forefathers did, with a clear conscience, as night and day I constantly remember you in my prayers. ⁴ Recalling your tears, I long to see you, so that I may be filled with joy. ⁵ I have been reminded of your sincere faith, which first lived in your grandmother Lois and in your mother Eunice and, I am persuaded, now lives in you also. ⁶ For this reason I remind you to fan into flame the gift of God, which is in you through the laying on of my hands. ⁷ For God did not give us a spirit of timidity, but a spirit of power, of love and of self-discipline.*

*⁸ So do not be ashamed to testify about our Lord, or ashamed of me his prisoner. But join with me in suffering for the gospel, by the power of God, ⁹ who has saved us and called us to a holy life—not because of anything we have done but because of his own purpose and grace. This grace was given us in Christ Jesus before the beginning of time, ¹⁰ but it has now been revealed through the appearing of our Savior, Christ Jesus, who has destroyed death and has brought life and immortality to light through the gospel. ¹¹ And of this gospel I was appointed a herald and an apostle and a teacher. ¹² That is why I am suffering as I am. Yet I am not ashamed, because I know whom I have believed, and am convinced that he is able to guard what I have entrusted to him for that day.*

*¹³ What you heard from me, keep as the pattern of sound teaching, with faith and love in Christ Jesus. ¹⁴ Guard the good deposit that was entrusted to you—guard it with the help of the Holy Spirit who lives in us.*

*2 Timothy 1:3–14, NIV*

1. At what point(s) can you identify with Timothy in this passage?
   - ❑ I had (have) a spiritual mentor like Paul
   - ❑ I am the object of my parents' constant prayers
   - ❑ I inherited faith from my parents/grandparents
   - ❑ I cry easily when saying goodbye to close friends
   - ❑ I have a spiritual gift which needs rekindling
   - ❑ I possess God's power, love, and self-discipline
   - ❑ I have been entrusted with great spiritual responsibility

2. If you had received a letter like this from an older Christian, how would you have felt?
   - ❑ challenged
   - ❑ thankful
   - ❑ inspired
   - ❑ patronized
   - ❑ loved
   - ❑ offended
   - ❑ angry
   - ❑ other: _____

3. Why did Paul refer to the faith of Timothy's mother and grandmother?
   - ❑ to remind Timothy to be a "good boy" and do the same
   - ❑ to remind Timothy of his heritage of faith
   - ❑ to compliment Timothy by complimenting his family
   - ❑ to impress Timothy with his memory of names

4. Who were the people in your family who (like Lois and Eunice for Timothy) inspired you to faith? Who has been a mentor to you (like Paul was to Timothy)?

5. What did Paul mean when he told Timothy to "fan into flame the gift of God" that was within him?
   - ❑ maybe he had heartburn
   - ❑ he needed to increase his faith
   - ❑ he needed to nurture and develop his gifts
   - ❑ he needed more of the Holy Spirit in his life

6. What did Paul mean when he said, "God did not give us a spirit of timidity"?
   - ❑ it's wrong to be shy
   - ❑ God wants us to be bold risk-takers
   - ❑ God doesn't want us to be held back by our fears
   - ❑ it's OK to be timid in general, but it's not helpful for ministry

7. In which situations are you most likely to have a "spirit of timidity"?
   - ❑ in being with the opposite sex
   - ❑ in meeting strangers
   - ❑ in social situations in general
   - ❑ when it comes to taking professional risks
   - ❑ in confronting people with whom I have a conflict
   - ❑ in leading or speaking to groups
   - ❑ in testifying for Christ without being "ashamed" (v. 8)
   - ❑ other: _____

8. What would it mean for you to have a spirit of "power, love and self-discipline" in the situation you described in question #7?

9. What would you have to do to "fan into flame the gift of God that is within you"?
   - ❐ be more in touch with the Holy Spirit
   - ❐ get more training to develop my gifts
   - ❐ use my gifts more in serving God and others
   - ❐ get more encouragement from others in the use of my gifts

LEADER: When you have completed the Bible study, move on to the Caring Time (below).

10. Imagine that you truly put aside your "spirit of timidity" and acted in a spirit of "power, love and self-discipline." How would you use your gifts in service to God and others?

# CARING TIME / 20 Minutes / All Together

*Leader: Bring all of the foursomes back together for a time of caring. Follow the three steps below.*

**SHARING**

One of the best ways to figure out what God wants you to do with your life is to take a look at your abilities and assets. Finish the sentence by checking three or four things: "I am good at..."

- ❐ working with children
- ❐ working with older people
- ❐ getting others involved
- ❐ helping behind the scenes
- ❐ making people laugh
- ❐ peacemaking/reconciling
- ❐ problem solving
- ❐ cheering others on
- ❐ teaching the Bible
- ❐ organizing/administrating
- ❐ being sensitive to others
- ❐ helping others start a business
- ❐ sharing my faith
- ❐ motivating/leading
- ❐ listening/caring
- ❐ playing sports
- ❐ crusading for a cause
- ❐ playing an instrument
- ❐ sticking it out
- ❐ cooking/homemaking
- ❐ coaching/teaching
- ❐ hanging out with kids
- ❐ running a business
- ❐ acting/singing
- ❐ raising money
- ❐ other: _____

If you knew you could not fail, what is one thing you would like to give your life to? Take some time to share any personal prayer requests.

**PRAYER**

Close with a short time of prayer, remembering the requests that have been shared. If you would like to pray in silence, say the word "Amen" when you have finished your prayer, so that the next person will know when to start.

**ACTION**

Choose one of your gifts and use it in a new way this week—for others or for God. Note the results, both in terms of how others are affected and how you feel about using your gift in this new way.

**v. 14**  **it will be like**... "It" refers to the kingdom of heaven (see Mt. 25:1). The kingdom starts here and now with responsible stewardship. Wealthy people entrusted their resources to servants, who acted as managers of the estate in their absence.

**v. 15**  **five talents**... "Talent" originally referred to a measure of weight. It became a monetary measure, equal to about $1,000 in silver or gold. It would take a laborer almost twenty years to earn one talent! **each according to his ability**... Each would be evaluated only in terms of what had been entrusted to him.

**vv. 16–18**  Two of the servants had very good returns on their investments. The third servant failed to do anything constructive with his portion. **dug a hole**... In the absence of safe deposit boxes, this was a common way to protect money. However, its investment possibilities were nil!

**v. 19**  **After a long time**... The indefinite time reference reminds the disciples that the final coming of the kingdom is still far off. **settled accounts**... This was the time of reckoning in which the master would evaluate how the various servants had fulfilled their responsibility.

**vv. 20–23**  The first two servants receive warm commendation from their master. Their faithfulness allows the master to trust them with greater responsibility. The servants welcome the master's inspection, because they know they have done a good job. **few things/many things**... They are rewarded with greater administrative responsibility in the master's household. The point is that the talents are "a few things" in comparison with the responsibility with which these servants will now have. **Come and share your master's happiness**... The servants are invited into a new relationship with the master—his friendship and respect.

**v. 21**  **a hard man**... The description of the master is uncomplimentary: it pictures him as harvesting for himself the fruits for which other people have worked. The listeners (who were poor) might naturally be inclined to favor the servant over a "hard" rich man. But nothing in the story indicates that the servant's characterization of the master was correct. He was generous in entrusting his property to the servants. And he was generous to the first and second servants upon his return. The question is raised in the listeners' minds as to whether the servant was correct or just irresponsible in light of such a generous master's trust.

**vv. 24–25**  This servant's reason for hiding the money was based on his fear of failing to live up to the master's high expectations. Rather than risk having to make up any loss he may have incurred by making a bad investment, he simply planned on returning the money. **here is what belongs to you**... Rabbinic teaching emphasized that God had given Israel the responsibility to protect the Law until he established his kingdom. Jesus may have this tradition in mind with this parable. While the Pharisees have "protected" the law from being corrupted by the masses, they have failed to use it in a way that would draw others to God. They can only return it to God intact, but without showing any benefit from having been entrusted with it. Thus, their judgment is assured.

**vv. 26–27**  The servant stands condemned by his own words. Whether or not his assessment of the master was correct, he should have at least tried to make some safe investments, so that there would be at least a small profit.

v. 26 **you wicked, lazy servant**... The master turns the tables on the servant. His action did not betray a wise fear of the master's authority, but simply a neglect of his responsibility. **I harvest where I have not sown**... While this is meant to be a parable of what God has entrusted to us, we must be careful not to make too exact a comparison between God and this miserly master. A parable is meant to have one central point. In this case, it is that what God gives us, he gives us to use responsibly. There was no intent to make all the comparisons exact. We should not then try to argue from this parable that God is harsh and greedy. Jesus gave his life to show just the opposite—that God's love and grace is abundant!

v. 27 **on deposit**... Lit. "on the table"—the table used by money changers in Jerusalem. All financial dealings in the temple had to be conducted in local currency. Therefore, one was guaranteed at least some interest would be earned.

vv. 28–30 Judgment is pronounced on this servant. He loses the capital he had been given, while it is added to the interest of the most faithful servant. The parable is meant to warn the disciples to apply themselves to the task of serving Jesus with all diligence. God expects those to whom he has entrusted various gifts to be faithful in their use of them for his purposes.

v. 29 **everyone who has/whoever does not have**... Those who hear and practice the word from God (that they have been given) are those who will be able to understand and receive more from God. Those who neglect what they have already heard will not be given any more.

v. 30 **weeping and gnashing of teeth**... A stock phrase used to indicate extreme horror and suffering. This does not describe what happened to the servant in the parable, but what will happen to the one who does not use what God has given them in service to him.

**Summary**... Paul reminds the younger Timothy of the gift of God within him, and urges him not to use it timidly. Rather, he is to use it with the spirit of power, love, and self-control which God has given. This especially means to be unashamed of witnessing for Christ.

**REFERENCE NOTES:
2 TIMOTHY 1:3–14**

vv. 3–5 **as my forefathers did**... In contrast to the false teachers who had, effectively, left the faith, Paul stands squarely in the tradition of his OT forebears. **recalling your tears**... Paul is probably remembering when they parted the last time—he to go on to Macedonia, while Timothy stayed in Ephesus. **grandmother/mother**... Nothing is really known of Timothy's grandmother, except what is written here. Acts 16:1 tells us that Timothy was from a town called Lystra. His mother was "a Jewess and a believer," but his father was a Greek. Normally a Jewess would not marry a Greek, because the family would ostracize her. However, Eunice and her family may not have been committed Jews when the marriage occurred. There is no mention of the father's faith.

v. 6 Paul turns from thanksgiving to exhortation. **fan into flame**... There is a strong connection in Scripture between the Spirit, the gifts of the Spirit, and fire. This image of "fanning into flame" presumes the "fire" is already there, but needs to be tended and nurtured. **laying on of my hands**... The Holy Spirit was conveyed symbolically on a new Christian when Christian leaders laid hands on the person and prayed. **fan into flame**... Lit.

"rekindle." Paul uses the image of a fire not to suggest that the gift of ministry has "gone out," but that it needs constant stirring up (so that it always burns brightly). **the gift of God**… Paul reminds Timothy not only of his spiritual roots (the faith of his mother and grandmother), but of the gift (*charisma*) he has been given for ministry.

v. 7  **timidity**… "The translation 'timid' is probably too weak. The word, often appearing in battle contexts, suggests 'cowardice.' " (Fee). **power/love/ self-discipline**… The gift the Spirit gave Timothy leads not to "timidity," but to these positive characteristics.

v. 8  **his prisoner**… Paul probably wrote this from a jail in Rome, where he had been put on suspicion of supporting a king other than Caesar. Timothy is able to do what Paul here calls him to do, because he has been given the gift of power, love, and self-discipline (v. 7). **ashamed to testify about our Lord**… The gospel message about a dying Savior was not immediately popular in the first-century world. The Greeks laughed at the idea that the Messiah could be a convicted criminal, and that God was so weak that he would allow his own son to die. The Jews could not conceive of a Messiah (whom they knew to be all-powerful) dying on a cross (which they felt disqualified him from acceptance by God). **ashamed of me**… When Paul was arrested, his friends deserted him (see v. 15). He does not want Timothy to do the same. **his prisoner**… Paul may be in a Roman jail, but he knows that he is not a prisoner of Caesar—but a willing prisoner of Jesus (Eph. 3:1; 4:1; Phm. 1, 9). **suffering**… Paul understands from his own experience (and from that of Jesus) that suffering is part of what it means to follow the gospel.

vv. 9–10  Paul reminds Timothy of the content of the gospel. The glorious nature of the gospel will bolster Timothy's confidence and will give him a strong reason not to be ashamed of it. **holy life**… "Holy" means living a life that is dedicated to God. Jesus taught that holy living was concerned with the needs of people, not with "acting religious." **grace**… God's work of salvation depends wholly on grace (his unmerited favor lavished on his creation)—not on "anything we have done." This grace, which was in place from "the beginning of time," is "given us in Christ Jesus" (see Eph. 1:4). **appearing**… The Greek word is *epiphaneia* (from which the English word "epiphany" is derived). It refers here to the manifestation of God's grace through the incarnation of Christ. **Savior**… This was a common title in the first century. It was applied to the Roman emperor (in his role as head of the state religion), and to various redeemer-gods in the mystery religions. Christians came to see that Jesus was the one and only Savior. **death/life**… Jesus' work of salvation is described in his twofold act of destroying the power of death over people, and bringing resurrection life in its place.

vv. 11–12  It is for the sake of the gospel that Paul is now in prison—a further reason why Timothy ought not to be ashamed of him. **herald/apostle/ teacher**… "The apostles formulated the gospel, preachers proclaim it like heralds, and teachers instruct people systematically in its doctrines and in its ethical implications" (Stott). **I am not ashamed**… The fact that he is in prison brings no shame to Paul, despite how others might view it.

vv. 13–14  What Timothy has learned from Paul is the model for "sound teaching." Paul urges Timothy to faithfully preserve the "sound teaching" of the gospel (1:12; 1 Tim. 6:20).

# SESSION 5

# The Role of Money

**PURPOSE:** To discover the role of money in relation to our calling.

**AGENDA:**  Gathering 📖 Bible Study ♡ Caring Time

## GATHERING / 10 Minutes / All Together

*Leader: Continue to be sensitive to all who share. However, by this time, group members should feel comfortable enough with each other to share at a deeper level.*

**OPEN**

**Step One: A FEW QUICK C–NOTES.** Imagine that you are 14 years old again and a rich aunt or uncle just gave you $500. Decide how much you would put into each of the following categories. See if the group can guess which category each person put the most in:

| | |
|---|---|
| ____ clothes | ____ my hobby |
| ____ sports equipment | ____ candy and treats |
| ____ give to friends | ____ help with family needs |
| ____ trading cards | ____ go out with friends |
| ____ dates | ____ music |
| ____ savings | ____ skiing |
| ____ tickets to a rock concert | ____ church |

**INTRODUCTION**

**Step Two: THE ROLE OF MONEY.** In our society, what we do in life is tied very closely to the issue of money. Talk to a college student about what work he or she is pursuing. It's inevitable that one of the areas of conversation will be how much money the student plans to make. That is not entirely bad, as money is a relevant factor in our lives. We want to take care of our needs and the needs of our family. Also, money helps us support the church and others in need.

The problem comes when money becomes the primary factor in decision-making in our professional lives. Where we might make the most money is not necessarily where we will make our greatest contribution to the world. Where we make the most money is not necessarily where we will be most fulfilled as persons. And where we make the most money is not necessarily where God wants us to be.

**LEADER: Choose the Track One Bible study (page 41) or the Track Two study (page 43).**

In this session, we will consider the role of money in relation to our calling. In Track One, we will look at Jesus' teaching in his most famous sermon, the Sermon on the Mount (Matthew 6:19–24), and what it has to say about money. Then in Track Two, we will consider what Paul (in his first letter to Timothy) has to say about the evil an excessive love of money can bring to life.

# BIBLE STUDY / 30 Minutes / Groups of 4

*Leader: Help the group choose a Track for study. Divide into groups of 4 for discussion. Remind the Convener for each foursome to move the group along so the Bible Study can be completed in the time allotted. Have everyone return together for the Caring Time for the final 20 minutes.*

**Track 1**

## True Treasure
## Matthew 6:19–24

**STUDY**

This passage is part of what is generally called Jesus' "Sermon on the Mount." In it, he focuses on practical wisdom about how to live life. Read Matthew 6:19–24, and discuss the questions which follow with your group. If you have difficulty with a word or phrase, consult the Reference Notes on pages 46–47.

> ¹⁹ *"Do not store up for yourselves treasures on earth, where moth and rust destroy, and where thieves break in and steal.* ²⁰ *But store up for yourselves treasures in heaven, where moth and rust do not destroy, and where thieves do not break in and steal.* ²¹ *For where your treasure is, there your heart will be also.*
> ²² *"The eye is the lamp of the body. If your eyes are good, your whole body will be full of light.* ²³ *But if your eyes are bad, your whole body will be full of darkness. If then the light within you is darkness, how great is that darkness!*
> ²⁴ *"No one can serve two masters. Either he will hate the one and love the other, or he will be devoted to the one and despise the other. You cannot serve both God and Money."*
>
> *Matthew 6:19–24, NIV*

1. Imagine that you are covering this part of the "Sermon on the Mount" for the financial section of the *Jerusalem Times*. What headline might you give your article?
   ❏ Prophet Promotes Foreign Investing
   ❏ Famous Rabbi Bullish on Heaven
   ❏ Securities not so Secure, Says Teacher
   ❏ Religious Fanatic Undercuts Economy—Berates Money
   ❏ Apostle Asks, "Why Seek to Get Rich in this Life, When You Can't Take it with You to the Next?"

*"...we need instruction on how to possess money without being possessed by money."*
*—Richard Foster*

2. What do you see as the main implication of Jesus' teaching for today?
   ❏ anyone who has more than I do is un-Christian
   ❏ we should sell everything and become monks
   ❏ we should live a simplified lifestyle, with only minimal possessions
   ❏ possessions are bad if they keep us from tithing and giving to help others
   ❏ every purchase must be weighed against our investments in God's kingdom
   ❏ other: _____

3. What was your most prized possession when you were:
   7 years old: _____
   14 years old: _____
   18 years old: _____
   now: _____

4. In what way have you used one of the possessions you mentioned above (in question #3) to help bring joy to others?

5. In Jesus' day, to say that a person had a "bad eye" meant that he or she was stingy. From verses 22–23, what does Jesus imply about the fate of someone whose lifestyle is marked by greed rather than generosity?
   ❐ they will be happier because they have more
   ❐ they are basically good people, but have a blind side
   ❐ their greed permeates their entire being
   ❐ they are eternally doomed
   ❐ other: _____

6. On the scale below, evaluate how you think the following groups are doing on the issue of serving God or serving money:

| 1 | 2 | 3 | 4 | 5 | 6 | 7 | 8 | 9 | 10 |
|---|---|---|---|---|---|---|---|---|----|
| **serving money** | | | | **trying to do both** | | | | | **serving God** |

   ___ what most people in our country are doing
   ___ what most church members in our country are doing
   ___ what most of my friends are doing
   ___ what I am doing

7. Imagine that you are going to Heavenly Securities Investment Corporation (HSIC) to open a new investment portfolio. The first question they ask is, "What is your main investment objective?" How do you answer?
   ❐ to invest enough to get rid of this guilt I'm beginning to feel
   ❐ to make sure I am investing in what lasts
   ❐ to get to heaven
   ❐ to please God
   ❐ other: _____

8. The investment counselor at HSIC shows you a variety of investment options that will allow you to "store up for yourself treasures in heaven." She asks you to prioritize them according to which you would like to add first to your portfolio, which second, etc. How would you prioritize them?
   ____ give more money to the church
   ____ give more money to people in need
   ____ give more time to the church
   ____ give more time to people in need
   ____ spend more time sharing my faith
   ____ get into a profession where I can use my gifts for people
   ____ give time to community work for human need
   ____ give more time to my family

*"Materialism is more than just our tendency to buy more than we should. It's our tendency to buy a false worldview which places material things at the center of life."*
—James Paternoster

42

**LEADER: When you have completed the Bible study, move on to the Caring Time (page 46).**

9. What is stopping you from investing in the prioritized areas you mentioned in question #8?
   - ❏ a lifestyle focused on materialism
   - ❏ unwillingness to take control of my time
   - ❏ lack of encouragement from others
   - ❏ lack of money or resources
   - ❏ nothing—I'm already doing so
   - ❏ nothing—I will start tomorrow
   - ❏ other: _____

10. What are some potential pitfalls in pursuing wealth?

11. What attitudes or actions might have been different this week if you were primarily concerned with laying up treasure in heaven rather than on earth?

**COMMENT**

Please read the Comment at the end of Track Two on page 45.

# A Root of Evil
# 1 Timothy 6:3–10

**STUDY**

This letter is primarily concerned with false doctrine. And in this passage, we see some connection between such false doctrine and the false value of money. Read 1 Timothy 6:3–10, and answer the discussion questions which follow. Consult the Reference Notes on page 47 for a fuller understanding of the text.

*³ If anyone teaches false doctrines and does not agree to the sound instruction of our Lord Jesus Christ and to godly teaching, ⁴ he is conceited and understands nothing. He has an unhealthy interest in controversies and quarrels about words that result in envy, strife, malicious talk, evil suspicions ⁵ and constant friction between men of corrupt mind, who have been robbed of the truth and who think that godliness is a means to financial gain.*
*⁶ But godliness with contentment is great gain. ⁷ For we brought nothing into the world, and we can take nothing out of it. ⁸ But if we have food and clothing, we will be content with that. ⁹ People who want to get rich fall into temptation and a trap and into many foolish and harmful desires that plunge men into ruin and destruction. ¹⁰ For the love of money is a root of all kinds of evil. Some people, eager for money, have wandered from the faith and pierced themselves with many griefs.*

*1 Timothy 6:3–10, NIV*

*"Money is a terrible master but an excellent servant."*
*—P. T. Barnum*

1. Which of the following describes your initial reaction to this passage?
   - ❏ sounds like a "Bible thumper"
   - ❏ sounds like someone who is poor and jealous
   - ❏ this points out what is wrong with our country
   - ❏ this points out some things I have learned about the dangers of money
   - ❏ boy, do I know some people who ought to read this

2. What kind of person do you think of when this letter talks about people "who think that godliness is a means to financial gain" (v. 5)?
   - ☐ television evangelists
   - ☐ professional ministers in general
   - ☐ those who teach that financial success is a sign of God's favor
   - ☐ those who use church only as a business connection
   - ☐ business people who act religious while using cutthroat tactics

3. What would it mean for you to take seriously the teaching, "godliness with contentment is great gain" (v. 6)?
   - ☐ to focus less on what I want to get and more on who I want to be
   - ☐ to stop striving all the time for more things
   - ☐ to focus on God's will and spiritual gain
   - ☐ to appreciate my family and the riches in friendship

4. How do you feel about the idea: "We brought nothing into the world, and we can take nothing out of it" (v. 7)?
   - ☐ if I can't take it with me, I ain't goin'
   - ☐ I might not be able to take it with me, but it sure makes things nicer while I'm here
   - ☐ I took nothing in, I'm taking nothing out, and I haven't got anything while I'm here
   - ☐ that's why I invest in relationships—I *can* take those with me

5. In what ways should the fact that "we can't take it with us" influence the way we live (v. 7)?
   - ☐ we should be more giving to others in need
   - ☐ we should hoard and accumulate until right before we die
   - ☐ we should sit back and let God (and the government) take care of us
   - ☐ we should continually seek God's contentment and guidance for the way we spend money

6. How do you react to the idea of being content with food and clothing (v. 8)?
   - ☐ that was really just for poor first-century Christians who couldn't do any better for themselves
   - ☐ well, if the clothing is from Saks Fifth Avenue....
   - ☐ no way—I've got to have my toys
   - ☐ how about food, clothing, and *shelter*?
   - ☐ how about food, clothing, shelter, and *cars*—oh, yes, and antiques, and TVs, and VCRs, and home computers, and....
   - ☐ it sets a good principle—the simpler, the better

7. What do you think is the most serious temptation for the person who wants to get rich (v. 9)?
   - ☐ using people to get things
   - ☐ valuing money more than their vocation or God's will
   - ☐ believing that things give us security
   - ☐ always wanting more
   - ☐ other: _____

8. Which of these phrases (from recent popular songs) describes the attitude toward money that prevailed in your family when you were growing up?
   ❏ "I don't care too much for money: money can't buy me love"
   ❏ "We're living in a material world..."
   ❏ "Money talks... but I'd much rather be forever in blue jeans"
   ❏ "Fifty thou a year will buy a lot of beer"
   ❏ "...and it's going to take money, a whole lot of spending money... to make it right"
   ❏ "Who is rich and who is poor, and who has more than me? Miracles, miracles—that's what life's about"
   ❏ "...you load sixteen tons, what do you get? Another day older and deeper in debt"

9. Which of these evils have you found yourself involved in because of your desire for money?
   ❏ cheating on taxes
   ❏ padding expense accounts
   ❏ neglecting my family to earn a little more
   ❏ ignoring human needs, so I don't feel compelled to give
   ❏ compromising business ethics for profit
   ❏ hurting someone else's reputation in order to get ahead at work
   ❏ other: _____

10. In what way has our discussion in this session affected your search for your calling?
    ❏ I need to open myself to a profession that may not pay as much
    ❏ I need to realize that volunteer activities are valuable, even if they don't pay
    ❏ I need to see my present job as service and not just a way to make money
    ❏ I need to see that part of my calling is caring for my family

11. If you could reduce your financial commitments and simplify your lifestyle, would you do it? Why or why not? Where would you cut back if you decided to do so?

**LEADER: When you have completed the Bible study, move on to the Caring Time (page 46).**

**COMMENT**

Richard Foster defines commitment to Jesus as the discipline of *simplicity*—living for the kingdom of God (as opposed to the loyalties of the world). He writes that freedom from anxiety is characterized by three inner attitudes:
- to receive what we have as a gift from God
- to know that it is God's business to care for what we have
- to have our goods available to others

Foster says that simplicity is not only an inner attitude; it also has an outward expression. The questions below help us to examine our lifestyle and our priorities:

1. Do I buy things for their usefulness rather than for their status? Do I sometimes act as though my happiness is really tied up with owning a certain product? Do I attempt to stay within my means and avoid financing schemes?

45

2. Am I willing to reject anything that might produce an addiction in me (i.e., a sense that I could just not do without _____)?
3. Am I able to enjoy things without having to possess them as my own? In what ways am I learning the freedom of giving things away?
4. Am I appreciative of the beauty of creation?
5. Are honesty and integrity the distinguishing characteristics of my speech?
6. Am I free to reject anything (e.g., possessions or positions) that breeds the oppression of others?
7. Do I shun whatever would distract me from my #1 priority—to seek first God's kingdom and righteousness? Do I actively cultivate attitudes and actions that would help me in this pursuit?

# CARING TIME / 20 Minutes / All Together

*Leader: Bring all of the foursomes back together for a time of caring. Follow the three steps below.*

**SHARING**

In relation to money, share with the group where you need God's direction. It may be:
- ❏ in learning to use it as a servant of God
- ❏ in trusting God to help you meet your bills
- ❏ in examining the ethics of how you make money
- ❏ in keeping it out of the "driver's seat" of your life

**PRAYER**

Close with a short time of prayer, remembering people's requests on how they need God's guidance. If you would like to pray in silence, say the word "Amen" when you have finished your prayer, so that the next person will know when to start.

**ACTION**

Go through your checkbook records for the past three months and note how you have been spending money. What does this say to you about your values and who you are serving?

**REFERENCE NOTES:**
**MATTHEW 6:19–24**

**Summary...** Jesus advises us to focus on "investing" in heaven, rather than in earthly wealth and goods. He especially warns us that we can't have it both ways. We cannot truly serve God and at the same time worship money.

vv. 19–21 The pursuit of wealth or possessions as a means of trying to obtain security in life is incompatible with seeking God's kingdom. **treasures on earth**... These are any material treasures which, by their very nature, are subject to theft, corrosion, decay, and loss. **moth and rust**... Lit., "moths and eating" (Mounce). While rich, elaborate clothes were one mark of a person's wealth, they could be destroyed in moments by insignificant creatures—moths and mice. Hence the foolishness of orienting one's life around them. **treasures in heaven**... Disciples "store up" these treasures by an obedient way of life. These are activities that have eternal consequences. What people occupy themselves with reveals the intent and character of their motives.

vv. 22–23 As a light shows us the way through the darkness, so the eye allows us to see so that we can move and act freely. Both eye and heart are biblical metaphors which describe the principle that guides the way a person lives (Ps. 19:36–37). The image of an "evil eye" described people who were greedy or stingy. The "good eye" refers to people who have a generous spirit.

v. 24 The contrast here is between competing masters. **serve**... Lit., "to be a slave of." While a person today might work for two employers, no slave could belong to two owners. **hate**... This is a dramatic way of expressing the fact that loyalty to one master makes loyalty to another literally impossible. **Money**... This is an Aramaic word that means possessions. God calls his people to "have no other gods besides me" (Ex. 20:3). He will not tolerate divided loyalty from his people (Eph. 5:5). **Money**... The word is capitalized here because it is personified as a rival god. Our problems do not come when money is a mere thing to be used, but when we treat it as if it were God.

**Summary**... We should be aware of people who teach false doctrines. Such people not only bring dissension, but they are often out for money. Our attitude toward money should be one of being content with what we have (even if it is only basic food and clothing). Striving to be rich brings many evils (including luring us away from our faith), and brings many griefs to our personal lives.

**REFERENCE NOTES:
1 TIMOTHY 6:3–10**

v. 3 **false doctrine**... Paul returns to the theme with which he began his letter (1:3). The false teachers have departed from the teaching of Jesus (see also 1:10, 4:6).

v. 4 **unhealthy interest**... Lit., "being sick or diseased." This sort of "morbid craving" (Bauer) stands in sharp contrast to the sound (or "healthy") instruction of verse 3. **controversies**... The word refers to a sort of idle speculation. They were preoccupied "with pseudo-intellectual theorizings" (Kelly). **arguments**... Lit., a "battle of words" which springs from pride and leads to bitterness, suspicion, and moral degeneracy. **envy**... Controversy produces jealousy as people choose sides (see Gal. 5:21; Rom. 1:29). **malicious talk, evil suspicions**... This quarreling drives people to insult and question one another.

v. 5 **corrupt mind**... "Mind" refers to one's whole way of thinking. **robbed of the truth**... Such corruption results in the loss of the very truth of the gospel. **godliness is a means to financial gain**... Paul does not consider it wrong for a person to be paid for teaching (see 5:17–18). However, the main motivation of these false teachers is the money they make from doing so (3:3, 8).

vv. 6–8 This verse contrasts the last words in verse 5, with a play on words. The false teachers think godliness "is a way to become rich." They are right, since there *is* great profit (metaphorically) in godliness if one is satisfied with what one has and does not seek material gain. **contentment**... A favorite word of the Stoic philosophers, referring to one who is not affected by circumstances. **clothing**... The word translated "clothing" includes "shelter" also. What is meant by this verse is, then, "the basics."

vv. 9–10 **want to get rich**... The reference here is not to those who already are rich, but to those whose motive is to *become* rich. The desire to get rich results in ruin and destruction. **love of money**... This well-known verse is often misquoted as "money is the root of all evil." But the reference here is to the *love* of money. Money can bring good when it is used in the proper way. But the love of money always brings evil, as it puts money in the place of a god. **some. . . have wandered**... Some of the false teachers were probably once good leaders in the church. However, they were caught by Satan, became enamored with speculative ideas, and were pulled down by their love for money.

# SESSION 6

# Our Attitude Toward Work

**PURPOSE:** To look at our attitude toward work and its relationship to our calling.

**AGENDA:**  Gathering  Bible Study  Caring Time

## GATHERING / 10 Minutes / All Together

*Leader: Read the instructions for Step One and go first. Then read the Introduction and explain the choices for Bible study.*

**OPEN**

**Step One: OUR "UN-CALLING."** To recognize our calling, perhaps it might help to eliminate some lines of work we would *not* like to do first. We can refer to this as our "un-calling"! Look over the list below and decide which you would least like to do, and share it with your group:

- ❐ crowd control officer at a rock concert
- ❐ private tailor for Oprah
- ❐ organizer of paperwork for Congress
- ❐ scriptwriter for Barney and Baby Bop
- ❐ public relations manager for Madonna
- ❐ researcher studying the spawning habits of Alaskan salmon
- ❐ bodyguard for Rush Limbaugh on a speaking tour of feminist groups
- ❐ toy assembly person for a local toy store over the holidays
- ❐ middle high school principal
- ❐ nurse's aide at a home for retired Sumo wrestlers with Alzheimer's
- ❐ consistency expert for chewing gum manufacturer
- ❐ official physician for the National Association of Hypochondriacs

**INTRODUCTION**

**Step Two: OUR ATTITUDE TOWARD WORK.** Finding our calling is integrally related to our attitude toward work. For some people, work is a necessary evil. They dream of the day when they will win the lottery, and won't have to work anymore. Work done with that kind of attitude is particularly wearying, and is often of poor quality.

To search for our calling is to believe there is a type of work we can do with pleasure and satisfaction, because we enjoy what we are contributing. It is to believe that when we follow God's leading (in terms of life occupation), God will not lead us to work that makes us miserable. Instead, God will lead us to a job which makes us fulfilled and whole as persons. Thus, having a positive attitude toward the work we do derives from believing we are called

48

**LEADER: Choose the Track One Bible study (below) or the Track Two study (page 51).**

to do that work. And believing we are called to do our work requires faith in God, and God's leading of our lives. Richard Nelson Bolles (author of the most popular job-search book in print, *What Color is Your Parachute?*) writes, "It is no accident that so many of the leaders in the job-hunting field over the years... have also been people of faith. If you would figure out your Mission in life, you must be willing to think about God in connection with your job-hunt."

In this session, we will look at our attitude toward work and its relation to our calling. In the Track One study (from Matthew's Gospel), we will look at a parable Jesus told about some tenants who were irresponsible with the work they were assigned to do. In the Track Two study (from Peter's first letter), we will consider what it means to submit to bosses as part of our calling.

# BIBLE STUDY / 30 Minutes / Groups of 4

*Leader: Help the group choose a Track for study. Divide into groups of 4 for discussion. Remind the Convener for each foursome to move the group along so the Bible Study can be completed in the time allotted. Have everyone return together for the Caring Time for the final 20 minutes.*

## Stewards in Our Work
## Matthew 21:33–41

**STUDY**

The following is one of the parables which Jesus told about our role as stewards in God's kingdom. Read Matthew 21:33–41, and discuss the questions which follow with your group. If you have questions about words or phrases, consult the Reference Notes on pages 54–55.

> [33] *"Listen to another parable: There was a landowner who planted a vineyard. He put a wall around it, dug a winepress in it and built a watchtower. Then he rented the vineyard to some farmers and went away on a journey.* [34] *When the harvest time approached, he sent his servants to the tenants to collect his fruit.*
> [35] *"The tenants seized his servants; they beat one, killed another, and stoned a third.* [36] *Then he sent other servants to them, more than the first time, and the tenants treated them the same way.* [37] *Last of all, he sent his son to them. 'They will respect my son,' he said.*
> [38] *"But when the tenants saw the son, they said to each other, 'This is the heir. Come, let's kill him and take his inheritance.'* [39] *So they took him and threw him out of the vineyard and killed him.*
> [40] *"Therefore, when the owner of the vineyard comes, what will he do to those tenants?"*
> [41] *"He will bring those wretches to a wretched end," they replied, "and he will rent the vineyard to other tenants, who will give him his share of the crop at harvest time."*
>
> *Matthew 21:33–41, NIV*

1. Imagine that the events of this parable actually occurred and you were covering the event for the *Jerusalem Herald*. Which of the following headlines would you give your story?
   - ❏ "Work Stoppage Results in Bloodbath"
   - ❏ "Tenant Farmers Hijack the Farm"
   - ❏ "Union Leaders Disavow Connection to Violent Actions"
   - ❏ "Valiant Landowner Vows to Start Again After Losses"

2. What is your reaction to the way the landowner responded to this crisis?
   - ❏ he was too nice—he should have called in the cops right away
   - ❏ he was naive—he should never have sent his son to violent people
   - ❏ he was a poor manager—he should have supervised them all along
   - ❏ he was a good man who was victimized by immoral workers

3. What caused the tenants to renege on the terms of their lease?
   - ❏ a communist agitator convinced them they had a right to the land
   - ❏ they saw the wealth of the landowner and wanted the same lifestyle
   - ❏ they were lazy and decided this was an easier way to get money
   - ❏ they liked the feeling of power which violence brings

*"And what is it to work with love? It is to weave the cloth with threads drawn from your heart, even as your own beloved were to wear that cloth."*
—Kahlil Gibran

4. Which of the following phrases best describes the attitude these tenants showed toward work?
   - ❏ it's like war, and the boss is the enemy
   - ❏ it's all about money and the easiest way to get it
   - ❏ like Karl Marx said: the value of a product comes from labor, not capital
   - ❏ we work for ourselves, regardless of the needs of others

5. What did Jesus want to teach with this parable?
   - ❏ the boss always wins
   - ❏ we will be held responsible in the end for the work entrusted to us
   - ❏ the ones who killed the servants (OT prophets) and the son (Jesus) will be punished
   - ❏ God owns everything and we shouldn't try to take over

6. Who do you identify most with in this parable?
   - ❏ the landowner—I always have to deal with deadbeats at work
   - ❏ the tenants—I've always felt the workers should run the company
   - ❏ the servants who were beat up—I'm always caught between management and labor

7. How would you describe your situation at work right now?
   - ❏ it's like war, and the boss is the enemy
   - ❏ everyone there is out for him/herself
   - ❏ it's similar to the tenants—labor is plotting against management
   - ❏ what "labor and management"?—We're all one team
   - ❏ other: _____

8. How would you describe your attitude toward work right now?
   - ❏ it's a paycheck
   - ❏ it's drudgery
   - ❏ I'm not really into it—I'm not giving it my all
   - ❏ I'm giving my all—but I'm not getting much out of it
   - ❏ I'm giving my all, and find a lot of satisfaction in what I'm doing
   - ❏ I'm very fulfilled by my work

9. What change of attitude might help you find more fulfillment in your work?
   - ❏ to stop looking at my job in economic terms only
   - ❏ to stop looking at my boss as my enemy
   - ❏ to look at what I am contributing rather than at what I am getting
   - ❏ to look for ways God can use me in my job
   - ❏ to focus on the people I work with, and find how God can love them through me

**LEADER: When you have completed the Bible study, move on to the Caring Time (page 53).**

# Submission to Our Task
## 1 Peter 2:13–21

**STUDY**

The following passage has had a controversial history because it was used to support slavery prior to our Civil War. But in it, Peter simply advises submission to the authorities who are (rightly or wrongly) placed over us. Read 1 Peter 2:13–21, and discuss the questions which follow with your group. If you find any difficult words or phrases, consult the Reference Notes on page 55.

*¹³ Submit yourselves for the Lord's sake to every authority instituted among men: whether to the king, as the supreme authority, ¹⁴ or to governors, who are sent by him to punish those who do wrong and to commend those who do right. ¹⁵ For it is God's will that by doing good you should silence the ignorant talk of foolish men. ¹⁶ Live as free men, but do not use your freedom as a cover-up for evil; live as servants of God. ¹⁷ Show proper respect to everyone: Love the brotherhood of believers, fear God, honor the king.*
*¹⁸ Slaves, submit yourselves to your masters with all respect, not only to those who are good and considerate, but also to those who are harsh. ¹⁹ For it is commendable if a man bears up under the pain of unjust suffering because he is conscious of God. ²⁰ But how is it to your credit if you receive a beating for doing wrong and endure it? But if you suffer for doing good and you endure it, this is commendable before God. ²¹ To this you were called, because Christ suffered for you, leaving you an example, that you should follow in his steps.*

*1 Peter 2:13–21, NIV*

1. If you did not know this was a passage of Scripture, what kind of communication do you think it might be?
   - ❏ an intra-office memo from my boss (especially the part about slaves!)
   - ❏ a royal edict from medieval times
   - ❏ an excerpt from a sermon preached in the antebellum South
   - ❏ other: _____

2. What does it mean to you to "submit yourself to every authority instituted among men" (v. 13)?
   ❒ I'm always supposed to be good and do what I am told
   ❒ I should respect civil authorities
   ❒ everyone must answer to some human authority
   ❒ I'm not sure what it means... but I don't like it

3. When you were a child, how did your parents expect you to respond to their authority?
   ❒ salute and say, "Yes, Sir!" or "Yes, Ma'am!"
   ❒ do everything we were told without question
   ❒ do what we were told, but questions were OK to a point
   ❒ at least show we were listening
   ❒ if we survived the day and didn't kill anyone, it was OK with them
   ❒ they just wanted us to stay out of the way

4. Below are guidelines that Peter offers to help us relate to those who have power over us. Which one do you identify with the most?
   ❒ **submission**: You don't fight the power. You don't rebel against it. You don't resist it aggressively. You accept its reality.
   ❒ **voluntary submission:** You choose to accept it. You do not let anyone force you to be under it, but take the power of choice into your hands.
   ❒ **submission for the Lord's sake:** You submit because you are a child of God, and this is his way of dealing with oppressive powers.
   ❒ **submission based on the Lord's example:** You try to do what Jesus did when he was arrested, tried, and crucified. Even though he suffered unjustly and was guiltless, he did not retaliate.
   ❒ **respect everyone:** You treat all people with care and consideration. You honor those who are above you and those who are below you in standing. You choose to do this. Others do not force you to do so.
   ❒ **respect even those who mistreat you:** Give honor even to those who by their behavior do not deserve it. In other words, your true identity is found in God, not in external circumstances. You are "conscious of God," and this defines reality for you.

5. On the scale below, how would you score yourself in terms of how you respond to authority figures now?

| 1 | 2 | 3 | 4 | 5 | 6 | 7 | 8 | 9 | 10 |
|---|---|---|---|---|---|---|---|---|----|

   When you say "jump," I'll just ask "How high?"          I'm a rebel—don't tell me what to do!

6. How does your attitude toward authority relate to your work?
   ❒ that's why I'm self-employed
   ❒ that's why I'm often out of work
   ❒ my independence makes my opinion valued
   ❒ I'm a valued employee, because I cooperate with those in charge
   ❒ I don't get along with people at work, because they think I "kiss up" too much
   ❒ I'm not sure when to assert my opinion and when to do what I'm told

**7.** This passage states that part of our calling is a calling to suffer (v. 21). What does this mean?
- ❏ Christians can be good witnesses only when they are miserable
- ❏ no cause means much—unless you're willing to go through hardship for it
- ❏ we should follow our leader, and our leader suffered
- ❏ the war against evil is like any war—you have to be willing to tough it out

**8.** What is the relationship (if any) between Peter's words about suffering and your attitude toward work?
- ❏ God wants me to put up with work that makes me miserable
- ❏ I need to put up with the hard stuff in order to accomplish what God wants me to
- ❏ I can't always have it my way, but what is important is God's way
- ❏ all meaningful accomplishment requires sacrifice

**LEADER:** When you have completed the Bible study, move on to the Caring Time (below).

**9.** To whom (or to what) do you need to submit in order to have more meaningful work?
- ❏ my boss or supervisor
- ❏ a commitment to serving people
- ❏ a willingness to sacrifice to follow God's calling
- ❏ nothing and no one—I submit only to my vision

**COMMENT**

Peter speaks directly to the social situation in which these Asian Christians find themselves. In terms of civil authority (now that Christianity was an illegal religion), the government had begun to persecute them. To be a Christian was, by definition, to be a criminal. In terms of the slavery issue, many in the church were themselves slaves. And to be a slave was to be under the absolute control of your master.

The questions Peter deals with here are of enormous importance to those in our world today who are also weak and powerless. But we hear Peter's words in a different way from the people who originally heard him. We are privileged and powerful in comparison. However, there are countless Christians throughout the world who know what it means to be in a position of subjection—be it secular powers, religious authorities, relational structures, or economic realities. In many countries, for instance, the economic structure is such that you are a virtual slave to your employer (who can treat you as he wants). Christians all over the world experience restricted rights.

We are not without our own difficulties, of course. We may have a job that saps us, leaves us exhausted, and without enough money to survive. We may know what it means to be discriminated against by the powers that be (because of our color, our ethnic background, or our lack of money).

# CARING TIME / 20 Minutes / All Together

*Leader: Continue to encourage the group to share openly. At this time in our studies, people should feel more comfortable in their depth of sharing.*

**SHARING**

Share with your group one relationship you are having difficulty with at work. It can be a boss, a supervisor, or one of your co-workers. How would you like this relationship to change? If this relationship improved, how might that help you to fulfill your calling?

**PRAYER**     Pray for the relationships people have shared about. If someone is uncomfortable praying aloud, encourage them to pray silently. When they conclude their prayer, ask them to say "Amen" so the next person will know to continue.

**ACTION**     This week, examine any way in which you might be "robbing" from your employer. This might include such actions as: wasting time, not giving a project your full attention, wasting or "borrowing" supplies, etc. Seek God's guidance and strength on how you can be a better steward in your work.

**Track 1**

**REFERENCE NOTES:**
**MATTHEW 21:33–41**

**Summary**... Jesus tells a parable about a landowner who rented his land to some farmers while he was away. When he returned, he sent servants to collect his fruit, but they were beaten and killed. They did the same to his son. Jesus asserts that the wicked tenants would be destroyed because of their poor stewardship and rebellious ways, and that the land would be given to others. Jesus clearly asserts that the leaders of Israel (who have turned against both him and John the Baptist), have rejected God's messengers and his authority. They have tried to usurp that authority for themselves and now face the prospect of judgment.

v. 33  **landowner**... This person (representing God) has entrusted his land (all of creation) to us. **vineyard**... Jesus' image reminded the religious leaders of Isaiah's well-known poem (Isa. 5:1–7). There the vineyard symbolized Israel. Although planted and cultivated by God, Israel was a vineyard that produced only bad fruit. As a result, the landowner destroyed it. Using the same image, Jesus creates a significant difference: for Isaiah, the problem was that Israel was an unresponsive vineyard; Jesus emphasized that Israel's leaders were like evil tenants (who refused to acknowledge God's authority over them). **vineyard**... Grapes were a major crop in Israel. A vineyard was built with a wall around it to keep out animals, a pit in which to crush the grapes to make wine, and a tower where the farmer kept watch for robbers. **went away**... Jesus changes the Isaiah poem here in order to put the religious authorities in the spotlight. In Isaiah, God is the farmer who waits for the fruit which never appears. In this parable, God is the landlord who leaves his vineyard in the care of others who are responsible to him.

v. 34  **servants**... These represent the prophets whom God sent to tell people of their responsibilities to him. Many of them were abused and killed. **collect his fruit**... A sharecropping system. The farmer who rented the land paid his own expenses and returned from one-quarter to half the crop to the landlord. It was this portion that the servants were trying to collect.

vv. 35–39 The tenants refuse to listen to the servants, beating and killing them instead. The fate of the servants in this parable is similar to what happened to many of God's prophets. **he sent his son**... The landowner assumed the tenants would acknowledge the authority of his own son, the heir of the vineyard. The crowd would not have known the identity of the son in this story, yet Matthew's readers know that this is Jesus. **take his inheritance**... The arrival of the son was misunderstood by the servants as a sign that the landowner had died. By law, a piece of ownerless property could be kept by those who first occupied and cultivated it. Since the tenants assumed the land would be ownerless if the son was dead, they plotted to kill him in order to lay claim to the land for themselves.

v. 41 **other tenants**... The essence of this parable is that the Jewish people have not responded to the message God has given them. They have not been true to their call to share that message. Christ says that his message and kingdom would now be shared with Gentiles (the other tenants). This does not mean that Jews will be shut out, only that the message will no longer be given to those who do not respond with faithful stewardship.

v. 13 **submit yourselves**... A key concept through 3:7, this involves voluntary subordination in all spheres of human interaction. **for the Lord's sake**... All that is done should be done for the Lord's sake, not for one's self, or for the sake of the authorities. **every authority instituted among men**... Lit. "every human creature."

v. 14 **sent by him to punish**... This does not mean that all human authorities use their authority in the way God intends, or that one should obey their every edict. Sometimes their demands are contrary to the call of God (see Ac. 4:19). We must weigh the demands of those who are over us (whether in our work or in government) against the demands of Christ. Note that at the time this letter was written, the Roman Emperor was probably Nero—one who severely persecuted the Christians in Rome!

v. 15 **silence the ignorant talk**... Christians were often seen as opposing society, and as supporting anarchy in government. They taught an allegiance to a different, non-earthly king. But Peter wanted Christians to redeem their reputation by showing people that they respected human government, even though they held allegiance to a higher power.

vv. 16–17 Christ brought freedom to people who had been bound by either Jewish or pagan religious rules and regulations. While affirming this freedom, Peter cautions that it is not the same as license. Even though they are free from such rules, Christians are bound as "slaves of God." **Show proper respect to everyone**... This call to "esteem highly" is the controlling commandment in this section. "The concept of submission. . . comes very close in meaning to that of 'respect' (2:17; 3:7)" (Michaels). The "everyone" here includes women, slaves, and children—a revolutionary concept in the first-century world, where such people were treated as property. **Love the brotherhood**... It is necessary to go beyond respect to love when it comes to one's fellow Christians. **fear God**... This is not the fear of cringing from someone who is out to hurt you; it is the awe which is due someone with power and authority. **honor the king**... Freedom in Christ cannot become an excuse for neglecting one's responsibilities to earthly authorities.

v. 18 Since many church members were probably slaves, this issue was important. **Slaves**... This word refers to house servants. **submit yourself**... This is not a defense of slavery. Rather, Peter didn't want Christians to be seen as undermining society. Essentially, he said, "Since slavery is a reality, here is the best way to live under it." Peter counsels an attitude of willing service, which is modeled on Christ. **with all respect**... Lit. "with all fear." This is not fear toward the master, but reverence toward God.

v. 19 **unjust suffering**... Experiencing unjust suffering gives a person a special link with Christ, since he also experienced that kind of suffering. That doesn't mean we shouldn't work for justice. But there will be some situations we will simply have to accept. We do so with an awareness that Christ experienced great injustice on our behalf. Although Roman slavery was not as brutal as what prevailed in America, slaves were still the victims of unjust treatment.

## SESSION 7

# The Servant Mind

**PURPOSE:** To develop an attitude where we work to serve our world and the people around us.

**AGENDA:**  Gathering  Bible Study  Caring Time

## GATHERING / 10 Minutes / All Together

*Leader: This is the final session together. You may want to have your Caring Time first. If not, be sure to allow a full 25 minutes at the end of the session.*

**OPEN**

**Step One: THE RIGHT TOOLS.** One of the most important tasks for people who work with their hands is to recognize what the right tool is for the job. Over these past six sessions, we have done an important job—the job of building community while we explore our vocation. Every person in this group has been a "tool" who has been used in that building process. In silence, think about the members of this group. Jot down their name next to the "tool" that describes them during these sessions. Then ask one person to sit in silence while the others explain where they put that person's name. Then go to the next person and do the same until everyone has been affirmed.

_____ **the HAMMER:** The one who drove home a point that stuck with you.
_____ **the SAW:** The one who always cut to the heart of the matter.
_____ **the PLANE:** The one who was there to "smooth things over" when there was tension.
_____ **the GLASSES:** The one who helped us to see our work more clearly.
_____ **the BRACE:** The one who gave us support.
_____ **the HINGE:** The one who gave our group flexibility.
_____ **the LEVEL:** The one who brought in a good balance.
_____ **the HOT GLUE:** The one who helped us to stick together as a group.
_____ **the FINE SANDPAPER:** The one who put a smooth luster on us.

**INTRODUCTION**

**Step Two: THE SERVANT MIND.** When work is a means to self-aggrandizement, then each person is in it for themselves. The issues become: "What is easiest for me?"; "What will advance my well-being?"; and "How can I get more money out of this?" The results of such self-focus are problematical in several ways. First of all, it is bad for our society. Product reliability suffers because it is always easier for a worker to take a shortcut than to do the job right. Consumer needs are considered only when there is a commercial advantage to do so. Worker loyalty becomes a thing of the past. It is also bad, however, for us as individuals. We can no longer take pride in our work, and we no longer see what we do as meaningful.

The generation of the 1980s was called the "Me Generation." It was said then that what each person should seek is individual self-fulfillment. But many people found that search to be a dead-end street. The reason was that self-fulfillment can only come when we see our work as a meaningful contribution to something beyond our self. Pollster Daniel Yankelovitch closely monitored the attitudes of today's younger adults for some time. He found that younger adults are now moving away from a pure self-fulfillment perspective to a desire to give themselves to something beyond themselves—to serve others and their world.

LEADER: Choose the Track One Bible study (below) or the Track Two study (page 59).

What we need in our work, then, is a revival of the servant mind—an attitude where we work to serve our world and the people around us. In this session, we will consider what it means to have a servant mind. In Track One, we will consider the example Jesus gave his disciples when he washed their feet (John 13:2–17). In our Track Two study, we will consider how Jesus set an example for us by taking on the form of a servant (Philippians 2:3–11).

# BIBLE STUDY / 25 Minutes / Groups of 4

*Leader: Remind the Conveners to end their Bible Study time 5 minutes earlier than usual to allow ample time for your final Caring Time—deciding what the group will do next.*

# An Example of Servanthood
# John 13:2–17

**STUDY**

The following passage describes an event during the Last Supper which Jesus celebrated with his disciples. Read John 13:2–17 and discuss the questions which follow with your group. If you have any questions about words or phrases, consult the Reference Notes on pages 63–64.

> [2] *The evening meal was being served, and the devil had already prompted Judas Iscariot, son of Simon, to betray Jesus.* [3] *Jesus knew that the Father had put all things under his power, and that he had come from God and was returning to God;* [4] *so he got up from the meal, took off his outer clothing, and wrapped a towel around his waist.* [5] *After that, he poured water into a basin and began to wash his disciples' feet, drying them with the towel that was wrapped around him.*
> [6] *He came to Simon Peter, who said to him, "Lord, are you going to wash my feet?"*
> [7] *Jesus replied, "You do not realize now what I am doing, but later you will understand."*
> [8] *"No," said Peter, "you shall never wash my feet."*
> *Jesus answered, "Unless I wash you, you have no part with me."*
> [9] *"Then, Lord," Simon Peter replied, "not just my feet but my hands and my head as well!"*
> [10] *Jesus answered, "A person who has had a bath needs only to wash his feet; his whole body is clean. And you are clean, though not every one of you."* [11] *For he knew who was*

*going to betray him, and that was why he said not every one was clean.*

*¹²When he had finished washing their feet, he put on his clothes and returned to his place. "Do you understand what I have done for you?" he asked them. ¹³ "You call me 'Teacher' and 'Lord,' and rightly so, for that is what I am. ¹⁴ Now that I, your Lord and Teacher, have washed your feet, you also should wash one another's feet. ¹⁵ I have set you an example that you should do as I have done for you. ¹⁶ I tell you the truth, no servant is greater than his master, nor is a messenger greater than the one who sent him. ¹⁷ Now that you know these things, you will be blessed if you do them."*

*John 13:2–17, NIV*

1. What do you think motivated Jesus to perform the act of footwashing at this point in time?
   - ☐ the stench of dirty feet was ruining his supper
   - ☐ with everyone relaxed, it was a good time to teach them about servanthood before he died
   - ☐ he watched the disciples play power games among themselves
   - ☐ he wanted to show them his deep love for them
   - ☐ he wanted to give them a new model for their life together

2. Why did Simon Peter initially refuse to let Jesus wash his feet?
   - ☐ he thought one of the other disciples should do it
   - ☐ he didn't think he was worthy
   - ☐ he didn't want his hero to stoop to such lowly behavior
   - ☐ he thought it was too personal an act, and he felt embarrassed
   - ☐ he thought his feet were clean already
   - ☐ he didn't understand what Jesus was doing

3. When Jesus told his disciples that they should wash one another's feet, he meant:
   - ☐ their feet were so dirty they needed a second wash
   - ☐ footwashing should be a regular church observance, like Communion
   - ☐ they should be willing to do the lowliest tasks in service to others
   - ☐ no one should do all the servant-tasks—they should all share them

4. When you were in the seventh grade, what kind of servant-tasks were you expected to do around your house?
   - ☐ make my bed             ☐ clean my room
   - ☐ look after younger siblings    ☐ cook
   - ☐ clean the dishes          ☐ laundry
   - ☐ yard work              ☐ vacuum
   - ☐ take out the trash        ☐ nothing
   - ☐ all of them—both of my parents worked

5. How did you feel about doing the tasks in question #4? What ingenious ways did you develop in order to avoid them?

6. What do you do for your family right now which is most like "washing feet"—a somewhat unpleasant, humble servant-task? How do you feel about doing this?

*"Jesus deliberately turned his back on all the ideas of power held in the world and proposed something new: servanthood."*
—Arthur M. Adams

*"Service means saying no to the power games of modern society."*
—Richard Foster

*"In God's family there is to be one great body of people: servants. In fact, that's the way to the top in his kingdom."*
—Charles Swindoll

7. What do you do at your job that is most like "washing feet"? How does Jesus' example affect your attitude about this task?

8. Which of the following is true with relationship to your present job and servanthood?
   ❑ my job has nothing to do with serving—it's about making money
   ❑ my job requires many servant-tasks, but most of them are pleasant
   ❑ my job requires many servant-tasks, most of which are not pleasant
   ❑ the main pleasure I get from my job comes from serving people
   ❑ I chose my job specifically so I wouldn't have to do unpleasant tasks like that

**LEADER: When you have completed the Bible study, move on to the Caring Time (page 61).**

9. What would it mean for you to take on the servant-mind of Christ in relation to your present profession (or in choosing your profession)?
   ❑ sounds like I would have to choose something unpleasant
   ❑ I would have to change the attitude with which I do most of my work
   ❑ I would focus more on the needs of people than on money and prestige
   ❑ I would have to realize that my self-fulfillment can only come if I am committed to serving others
   ❑ I would have to do a lot of things I'm not willing to do right now

Track 2

# Taking on Servanthood
## Philippians 2:3–11

**STUDY**

Throughout his letters, Paul takes care to not be seen as boastful or self-serving, but to be seen as a servant of Christ. In the following passage, he advises his readers to do the same thing by imitating Christ. Read Philippians 2:3–11 and discuss the questions which follow. If you do not understand a word or phrase, consult the Reference Notes on page 64.

³ *Do nothing out of selfish ambition or vain conceit, but in humility consider others better than yourselves.* ⁴ *Each of you should look not only to your own interests, but also to the interests of others.*
⁵ *Your attitude should be the same as that of Christ Jesus:*

⁶ *Who, being in very nature God,*
    *did not consider equality with God something to be grasped,*
⁷ *but made himself nothing,*
    *taking the very nature of a servant,*
    *being made in human likeness.*
⁸ *And being found in appearance as a man,*
    *he humbled himself*
    *and became obedient to death—*
        *even death on a cross!*
⁹ *Therefore God exalted him to the highest place*
    *and gave him the name that is above every name,*

*¹⁰ that at the name of Jesus every knee should bow,
in heaven and on earth and under the earth,
¹¹ and every tongue confess that Jesus Christ is Lord,
to the glory of God the Father.*

**Philippians 2:3–11, NIV**

1. How would you describe your initial reaction to this passage?
   - ❐ "Oh, Lord, it's hard to be humble when you're perfect in every way"
   - ❐ sounds like it encourages groveling to me
   - ❐ it's a beautiful and poetic description of the example Jesus set for us
   - ❐ it's OK for Jesus, but people can't do that and maintain their self-worth

2. How would your profession be affected if the people in it followed Paul's teaching, "Do nothing out of selfish ambition or vain conceit..."?
   - ❐ it would destroy our only motivation to excel
   - ❐ it would destroy business
   - ❐ it would make for a much more pleasant work experience
   - ❐ it would make us a tighter-knit work force
   - ❐ it would improve our service (or product)

Use the following scale for questions #3–#6:

| 1 | 2 | 3 | 4 | 5 | 6 | 7 | 8 | 9 | 10 |
|---|---|---|---|---|---|---|---|---|---|
| **My own interests always first** | | | | | | | | **The interests of others always first** | |

3. From this passage (and your own understanding), where do you think the best balance is between "looking to your own interests" and "looking to the interests of others" (v. 3)? _____

4. Where do you think the attitude of most people you work with (or go to school with) lies? _____

5. What attitude prevailed in the home where you were raised? _____

6. Judging by your present lifestyle, what score would you give yourself? _____

7. Which of the following ways in which Jesus displayed humility is the hardest for you to understand?
   - ❐ he took on the role of a servant
   - ❐ he didn't expect praise or recognition from others
   - ❐ he did everything in secret
   - ❐ he humbled himself and came to earth as a baby—the incarnation
   - ❐ he humbled himself to the point of death—death on the cross

8. What does this description of Jesus imply for the way we should live?
   - ❐ we should consider ourselves unimportant little nothings
   - ❐ nobody is too good to serve others
   - ❐ we shouldn't worry so much about status
   - ❐ God will exalt the person who humbles himself or herself

9. If you embraced the attitude of Christ, how would that affect your present job?
   □ I would have to leave it
   □ it would eventually get me fired
   □ it might cut our profit, but it would improve our service
   □ it would make my work more meaningful
   □ it would make me more sensitive to the people I work with and serve
   □ other: _____

10. Our Scripture refers to the goal that "every tongue confess that Jesus Christ is Lord." In all honesty, who (or what) are you declaring as "Lord" in the way you do your work?
   □ money               □ power
   □ my boss             □ status/prestige
   □ me                  □ early retirement
   □ my co-workers       □ financial security
   □ Jesus Christ        □ other: _____

LEADER: When you have completed the Bible study, move on to the Caring Time (below).

# CARING TIME / 25 Minutes / All Together

*Leader: This is decision time. These four steps are designed to help you evaluate your group experience and to decide about the future.*

**EVALUATION**

Take a few minutes to review your experience and reflect. Go around on each point and finish the sentences.

1. What key lessons have you learned about your gifts and calling in life from this series of Bible studies?

2. As I see it, our purpose and goal as a group was to:

3. We achieved our goal(s):
   □ completely          □ almost completely
   □ somewhat            □ we blew it

4. The high point in this course for me has been:
   □ the Scripture exercises
   □ the sharing
   □ discovering myself
   □ belonging to a real community of love
   □ finding new life and purpose for my life
   □ the fun of the fellowship

5. One of the most significant things I learned was...

6. In my opinion, our group functioned:
   □ smoothly, and we grew
   □ pretty well, but we didn't grow
   □ it was tough, but we grew
   □ it was tough, and we didn't grow

**7.** The thing I appreciate most about the group as a whole is:

**CONTINUATION**

Do you want to continue as a group? If so, what do you need to improve? Finish the sentence:

"If I were to suggest one thing we could work on as a group, it would be..."

**MAKE A COVENANT**

A covenant is a promise made to each other in the presence of God. Its purpose is to indicate your intention to make yourselves available to one another for the fulfillment of the purposes you share. In a spirit of prayer, work your way through the following sentences, trying to reach an agreement on each statement pertaining to your ongoing life together. Write out your covenant like a contract, stating your purpose, goals, and the ground rules for your group. Then ask everyone to sign.

**1.** The purpose of our group will be... (finish the sentence)

**2.** Our goals will be...

**3.** We will meet for _____weeks, after which we will decide if we wish to continue as a group.

**4.** We will meet from _____ to _____ and we will strive to start on time and end on time.

**5.** We will meet at _____ (place) or we will rotate from house to house.

**6.** We will agree to the following ground rules for our group (check):

    ❑ **Priority**: While you are in the course, you give the group meetings priority.
    ❑ **Participation**: Everyone participates and no one dominates.
    ❑ **Respect**: Everyone is given the right to their own opinion, and "dumb questions" are encouraged and respected.
    ❑ **Confidentiality**: Anything that is said in the meeting is never repeated outside the meeting.
    ❑ **Empty Chair**: The group stays open to new people at every meeting, as long as they understand the ground rules.
    ❑ **Support**: Permission is given to call upon each other in time of need at any time.
    ❑ **Accountability**: We agree to let the members of the group hold us accountable to the commitments which each of us make in whatever loving ways we decide upon.

**CURRICULUM**

If you decide to continue as a group for a few more weeks, what are you going to use for study and discipline? There are 15 other studies available at this 201 Series level. 301 Courses are for deeper Bible study, also with Study Notes.

For more information about small group resources and possible directions, please contact your small group coordinator or SERENDIPITY at 1-800-525-9563.

**Summary**... Jesus, while sharing in the Passover meal with his disciples, rises and begins to wash their feet. Peter objects, but Jesus says that if he does not wash Peter's feet, Peter will have no part of him. Jesus then tells his disciples to follow his example by serving others.

v. 2   **evening meal**... This was the Passover meal. It is the meal eaten in commemoration of when the angel of death passed over the children of Israel (during the plagues) that eventually helped to free them from Egypt.

vv. 3–5  **Jesus knew**... Jesus knew his own power, his own roots, and his own life direction. Knowing these things gives one the self-confidence to serve others. People who do not know these things must prove themselves by dominating others. **outer clothing**... By taking off this clothing, Jesus took on the appearance of a slave (who would normally do this work). Usually, people's dusty feet were washed by the lowest-ranking servant of the household. Jesus' action was deliberate. **wash his disciples' feet**... As the guests reclined at table (rather than sit in chairs as we do), the slave would come in front of the couch and wash their feet. Since none of the disciples would compromise his claim to honor by undertaking a servant's task, Jesus left the table and performed this menial duty.

vv. 6–8  **Lord, are you going to wash my feet?**... Peter, who recognized the impropriety of a Master washing his disciples' feet, protests. The Greek sentence actually reads more like "You? Wash *my* feet?" Peter is appalled by this break in normal procedure. **later you will understand**... This may simply refer to verse 17, but more likely it refers to the understanding of Jesus' servanthood that will be clearer after the resurrection. **Unless I wash you, you have no part with me**... This lifts the meaning of the footwashing to a higher plane than simply that of an object lesson about humility. Although it was not understood at the time, the image of being "cleansed" by Jesus became a common picture of what it meant to be forgiven of sin. Jesus' footwashing was a symbol of the spiritual cleansing he would accomplish for his followers through the cross. Peter needed to learn to be part of a community where people served each other.

v. 10  **A person who has had a bath**... Jesus uses the picture of a person, who, after washing completely, travels somewhere. Upon arrival, only his feet need be washed for him to be clean again. In 15:3, Jesus says the disciples are "already clean because of the word I have spoken to you." Their faith in Jesus' word may be the initial "bath" he refers to. After that, what they need is the ongoing "footwashing" of mutual forgiveness and love. **and you are clean, though not every one of you**... Lit. "though not all," which leaves the meaning ambiguous to the hearers. He may only mean that they are literally still not completely clean. But the context shows his real intent was to prepare them for his startling announcement in verse 21. **though not every one of you**... This was a veiled reference to Judas.

vv. 12–16  Jesus interprets his action for the disciples. They are to follow his example with each other without regard to titles or status. This will be the hallmark of the love to which he calls them. **"Teacher" and "Lord"**... These titles of respect for a rabbi were commonly used for Jesus. He acknowledges that they are appropriate to him. Yet, just as he laid aside the pretension of these titles in order to love others, so they should follow his example in expressing love for one another. **No servant is greater than his master**... In 15:20, he uses this phrase to prepare the disciples for the opposition they will face. Here, however, the phrase is meant to reinforce what he has just called them to do. If the master serves, how much more should the servants do so? **a messenger**... This is the same word as "apostle" (which only occurs here in this Gospel). An apostle was a person sent with the authority to represent the one who sent him. Jesus' followers are to represent his servanthood to others.

v. 17 **blessed**... "Happy" would be a better choice here. The word carries the sense of emotional joy that "happy" conveys. The mutual servanthood of the disciples will produce happiness in their community (precisely because it is concerned with the well-being of others). The only other "beatitude" in this Gospel is found in 20:29.

**REFERENCE NOTES:**
**PHILIPPIANS 2:3–11**

**Summary**... Paul urges his readers to act in humility and without selfish ambition. He points to Christ as an example. He did not insist on his right to heavenly glory, but instead took on human form as a servant. An essential way he served was by becoming obedient to the point of giving his life on the cross. While Christ humbled himself in this way, God's ultimate goal is for Christ to be exalted so that all will praise him.

vv. 3–4 **vain conceit**... Lit. "vain glory," asserting oneself over God (who alone is worthy of true glory). **humility**... Christians are to give others the same dignity and respect that Christ has given to all people. **better than yourselves**... This is not an instruction to be self-deprecating. All of us are God's children and worthy of honor. Rather, we are not to insist on our own rights and honor over the rights and honor of others. **look not only to your own interests**... Preoccupation with personal interests makes unity impossible (Rom. 15:1–3; Gal. 6:2).

vv. 5–11 Quoting from a hymn, Paul presents Jesus as the example of what self-sacrificing humility is all about. Verses 6–8 focus on the self-humiliation of Jesus, while verses 9–11 focus on God's exaltation of Jesus. **in very nature God**... Scripture (especially John 1:1–18) affirms that Christ was one with God from the beginning. Still, he did not hold on to that right so tightly that he was unwilling to humble himself and take on human form in order to serve and help people.

vv. 6–7 **being**... This word "describes that which a man is in his very essence, that which cannot be changed" (Barclay). **very nature**... This is "the essential form of something which never alters" (Barclay). Jesus Christ possesses the essential nature of God. **to be grasped**... Jesus did not have to "snatch" equality with God. It was his already, and thus he could give it away. **made himself nothing**... Lit. "to empty." **the very nature**... See above. **of a servant**... From being the ultimate master, Jesus became humanity's servant. **being made**... This verb points to the fact that at a *particular time* he was born as a human being.

v. 8 **in appearance**... This word denotes what is outward and changeable (over against that which is essential and eternal—v. 6). "His mankind was utterly real, but it was something which passed: the godhead was also utterly real, but it is something which abides forever" (Barclay). **he humbled himself**... This is Paul's central point. Jesus is the ultimate model of a life of self-sacrifice, self-renunciation, and self-surrender.

vv. 9–11 The self-humiliation of Jesus is followed by his exaltation through the resurrection and ascension. **name**... A name revealed the inner nature or character of a person. The name that was given to Jesus is "Lord"; Jesus is the supreme sovereign of the universe. **bow**... A quote from Isaiah 45:23. Jesus will receive the honor which in the OT was understood to be given to God alone. **Jesus Christ is Lord**... This, the climax of the hymn, is the church's earliest confession of faith.